TWENTY THINGS YOU NEED TO KNOW

Other Books by Donald J. Wheeler

Understanding Variation, the Key to Managing Chaos

Understanding Statistical Process Control

Making Sense of Data

EMP III, Evaluating the Measurement Process

The Six Sigma Practitioner's Guide to Data Analysis

Advanced Topics in Statistical Process Control

SPC at the Esquire Club

Normality and the Process Behavior Chart

Short Run SPC

Reducing Production Costs

Analyzing Experimental Data

Understanding Industrial Experimentation

You can get information about these
and other books by Dr. Wheeler,
at www.spcpress.com.

TWENTY THINGS YOU NEED TO KNOW

Donald J. Wheeler, Ph.D.
Fellow of the American Statistical Association
Fellow of the American Society for Quality
2010 Deming Medalist

SPC Press

Copies of this book may be obtained directly from SPC Press.

SPC Press
5908 Toole Drive, Suite C
Knoxville, Tennessee 37919
(865) 584-5005
Fax (865) 588-9440
(800) 545-8602
www.spcpress.com

ISBN 978 - 0 - 945320 - 68 - 5
x + 150 pages
58 figures
6 reference tables
13 data tables

2 3 4 5 6 7 8 9 10

CONTENTS

ABOUT THE AUTHOR

Donald J. Wheeler is a statistician who had the good fortune to work with both Dr. W. Edwards Deming and David S. Chambers. Dr. Wheeler graduated from the University of Texas, Austin, with a B.A. Degree in Physics and Mathematics, and holds M.S. and Ph.D. Degrees in Statistics from Southern Methodist University. From 1970 to 1982 he taught in the Statistics Department at the University of Tennessee, Knoxville, where he was Associate Professor. From time to time between 1981 and 1993 he was invited to assist Dr. Deming at his four-day seminars.

Dr. Wheeler is a Fellow of the American Statistical Association and a Fellow of the American Society for Quality. In 2010 he was awarded the Deming Medal "for excellence in the application of statistics in industry worldwide." He has conducted over 1100 seminars in seventeen countries on six continents. He is author or co-author of 25 books and over 250 articles. His books have been translated into five languages. Through these seminars and books Dr. Wheeler has had a profound impact on companies and organizations around the world.

PREFACE

The full title of this book ought to be "Twenty Things You Need to Know about SPC and Data Analysis Based on Lessons Learned in over Forty Years of Study, Practice, and Collaboration," but the space on the cover was a couple of light-years short to get it all in.

This book was conceived as a companion book for *Understanding Variation, The Key to Managing Chaos.* It provides brief answers to many of the commonly occurring questions that arise when people begin to use process behavior charts. While a few chapters will recap material from *Understanding Variation*, others will complement and complete the message of that book. In every case the objective was to enable you to better and more easily use process behavior charts to get the most out of your processes and operations. Chapter Ten has been extensively revised in this printing in the interest of greater clarity.

Since not all sources of information about SPC are equally reliable, some of the chapters will, of necessity, be focused on mistakes and misinformation that are currently in circulation. In the interest of completeness, these chapters will also include enough of the background material to justify the answer given. For additional documentation on the topics of each chapter of this book see the For Further Reading section of the Appendix. The books cited there include: *Understanding Statistical Process Control, Making Sense of Data, The Six Sigma Practitioner's Guide to Data Analysis, Advanced Topics in Statistical Process Control, Normality and the Process Behavior Chart,* and *EMP III Evaluating the Measurement Process.*

As always, it is my hope that you will find this book to be useful.

There is light enough
for those who wish to see,
and darkness enough
for those who are otherwise inclined.

Blaise Pascal

In this world
two plus two
is only equal to four
on the average.

David S. Chambers

CHAPTER ONE

THE TWO MISTAKES OF DATA ANALYSIS

In *Understanding Variation* the case was made that while some data may contain signals, all data contain noise. As a consequence of this reality, we cannot ever make sense of our data until we filter out the noise. And the primary tool for this filtration was shown to be a simple process behavior chart known as an *XmR* Chart.

If we fail to filter out the noise, we may interpret routine variation as if it is a signal. When we do this, we end up attributing the perceived change to nonexistent causes, with the inevitable consequence that our explanations will not fit the reality in which we have to work.

On the other hand, if we realize that some variation is merely routine, and do not properly separate the routine variation from the exceptional variation, then we may well end up missing some signals of change. When this happens we will fail to understand why the change has occurred, and an opportunity to gain knowledge will be missed.

Thus we have the two mistakes that we can make when we attempt to use data. Either we can interpret noise as a signal and chase after explanations that do not exist. Or, we can interpret a signal as a bit of noise and fail to learn that which could be learned.

As a consequence of these two mistakes, we find that the separation of signals from noise is fundamental to any and every form of data analysis. Analysis requires this separation, and any attempt to interpret data without analysis is an example of numerical naiveté. It is because of such naiveté that Mark Twain coined the phrase, "Lies, damned lies, and statistics." When people confuse noise with signals, anybody can make anything out of the data. If we do not filter out the noise, confusion is inevitable.

Unfortunately, many who are numerically naive do not recognize their naiveté. They think that because they can do arithmetic they are qualified to interpret data. Their approach can be summarized as: "Two numbers that are not the same are different!" This theorem of the unconsciously naive will turn everything into a signal, two points will always define a trend, and explanations will be required for all of the (unfavorable) noise in the monthly report.

The first step in avoiding this numerical naiveté is to understand the nature of the two mistakes of data analysis.

> **Mistake One:** Interpreting the routine variation of noise as if it amounted to a signal of a change in the underlying process, thereby sounding a false alarm.
>
> **Mistake Two:** Thinking that a signal of a change in the underlying process is merely the noise of routine variation, thereby missing a signal.

You can avoid Mistake One by refusing to believe that anything is a signal. While Dilbert's boss is never distracted by the data, and hence never makes Mistake One, he makes Mistake Two every day.

On the other hand, you can avoid Mistake Two by simply interpreting everything as a signal. The numbers go up, and that is a signal; the numbers go down, and that is a signal; the numbers stay the same, and that is a signal too because you expected them to go up or down. While this may keep you from ever missing a signal, you are very likely to be overwhelmed by Mistake One. A friend of mine once described a newspaper as having predicted 15 of the last three downturns in the stock market.

The trick is to strike a balance between the two mistakes by filtering out the noise of routine variation so that we can detect the potential signals within our data. This is the essence of effective data analysis.

CHAPTER TWO

TWO TYPES OF DATA

While the filtration of noise is the foundation of all data analysis, there are two distinct environments in which data analysis occurs. Some data are the result of an experiment or special study. Other data occur as a by-product of some operation. These two different environments for data analysis result in two different attitudes to the analysis itself. Since these differences are fundamental to a proper understanding and use of the techniques, we need to take the time to define the differences between Experimental Studies and Observational Studies.

EXPERIMENTAL STUDIES

When you do an experiment you will usually be comparing two or more conditions to determine which condition is, in some sense, better. A set of observations will be collected under each of the conditions, and these observations will form the basis of the comparisons. Since each condition will usually require special set-ups and dedicated runs, you will always have a limited amount of data to use in making the comparisons. This will affect the way in which you analyze these data. In particular, having just paid good money to create what you hope will amount to true signals of a difference, you will naturally want to detect any real differences that are present. Thus you will want a reasonably sensitive analysis in spite of the fact that you have a limited amount of data to use. Given these constraints, it is customary to accept a nontrivial risk of a false alarm. (Traditionally, this risk is known as the alpha-level and is commonly set at five percent.) With a one-time analysis, a five percent risk is generally small enough to allow us to interpret those differences that we detect as if they are real differences. Once we have detectable differences, then we can create a meaningful ranking for the conditions. (Without the detectable difference, any ranking may well be a meaningless ranking of noise.)

Thus, with an Experimental Study, we use a finite amount of data to perform a one-time analysis while looking for differences that we have tried to create by means of the experiment. To have a sensitive analysis we usually accept a non-trivial risk of a false alarm.

OBSERVATIONAL STUDIES

When the data are a by-product of operations you will usually be trying to operate the process in some steady state. Here you will usually want to know whether or not an unplanned change has occurred. This is a completely different question from the one considered with experimental data. Now only one condition is present, rather than two or more. *Here we are not looking for a difference that we think is there, but asking if an unknown change has occurred.* Before we sound an alarm we will want to be reasonably certain that a change has indeed occurred, making our approach to analysis conservative. Moreover, since a change can occur at any time, this question needs to be continually asked of the process. As each value is obtained you can use it to see if a change has occurred. This makes every point added to a chart into a separate act of analysis. Thus, an Observational Study, of necessity, requires a conservative, sequential analysis technique.

With a sequential analysis we risk having a false alarm with each new data point, and the only way to keep the overall risk of a false alarm from getting excessively large is to perform each individual act of analysis with a very small risk. While this may make each individual analysis fairly insensitive, with an Observational Study we have the luxury of waiting for the data to show any change that does occur. Hence, we can afford to perform each individual analysis with a trivial risk of a false alarm (usually a risk of less than one percent is preferred). In this environment, when we get a signal we can be reasonably sure that a change has indeed occurred in the process.

Thus, with an Observational Study, we perform a sequential analysis using a continuing stream of data while looking for signals of any unknown or unplanned change which may occur. To minimize false alarms we require a trivial risk of a false alarm for each individual act of analysis.

Thus, depending upon whether we have data from an Experimental Study or an Observational Study, the nature of the analysis changes, the questions asked by the analysis change, and the risks we take in the analysis change.

WHAT THIS MEANS IN PRACTICE

The fundamental differences between an Experimental Study and an Observational Study result in the use of different techniques and different approaches to analysis. A failure to understand these differences can result in confusion and inappropriate analyses.

Traditional classes in Statistics focus on Experimental Studies and the analysis techniques that are appropriate for this type of data. SPC is concerned with how to analyze the data from Observational Studies. When students, or even their instructors, fail to make a distinction between these two types of data, confusion is inevitable. This confusion is the source of many of the questions covered in this book. It is also a source of many traps, obstacles, and pitfalls that are set in the path of those seeking to use process behavior charts.

Confidence intervals, tests of hypotheses, and regression techniques are all designed to get the last ounce of information out of a fixed and finite amount of experimental data. Probability models and critical values are intended to sharpen up the analysis so no reasonable signal of a difference is overlooked. These are all tools for the analysis of data from Experimental Studies.

In contrast to all of the above, process behavior charts separate the potential signals from the probable noise by using generic and fixed three-sigma limits. Moreover, they allow us to perform this separation using data obtained under operational conditions, without the need to perform special experiments or studies. They are tools created for use in Observational Studies.

In Chapter Nine we shall look at another way in which the analysis of data from Experimental Studies differs from that from Observational Studies.

CHAPTER THREE

THE ORIGIN AND STRUCTURE OF VARIATION

Having made the distinction between routine variation and exceptional variation, it is helpful to have a conceptual model for the origins of these two different types of variation. To create this model we need to begin with a thought experiment. I would like for you to think of any single, measurable product characteristic or process outcome that you know something about.

Once you have selected this outcome characteristic, I would like for you to mentally list all of the possible cause-and-effect relationships that have an impact upon the measured value of your outcome characteristic.

In most cases your list will contain dozens, if not hundreds, of causes. Over time these lists of cause-and-effect relationships (and the accompanying cause-and-effect diagrams) can grow to be very large. I personally recall one that listed over 1300 causes for a single outcome characteristic.

Now, whether your list has dozens or hundreds of causes, it should be obvious that these different causes will not all have the same effect upon the outcome characteristic. Some causes will have large effects, while others will have small effects. If we had perfect knowledge and knew the effect of each cause upon our outcome characteristic, then we could arrange these causes in order of descending impact.

In most cases the result would look like the Pareto diagram shown in Figure 3.1. There the length of the bars represent the amount of variation introduced into the outcome characteristic by each of the 21 causes listed along the horizontal axis. As usual, the first few causes will contribute the lion's share of the variation. In Figure 3.1 the first four causes account for 79 percent of the variation in the outcome characteristic. By controlling these four causes we could eliminate 79 percent of the variation in the outcomes.

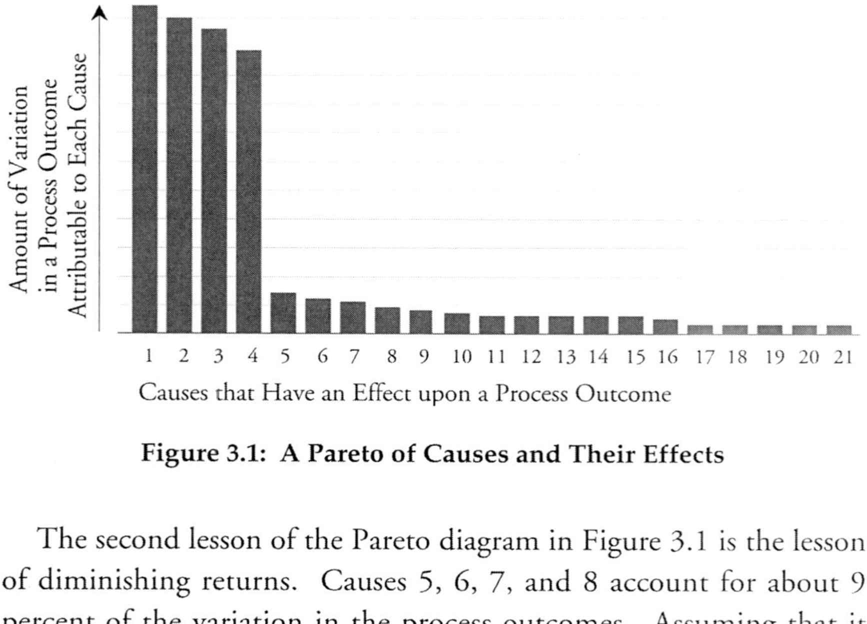

Figure 3.1: A Pareto of Causes and Their Effects

The second lesson of the Pareto diagram in Figure 3.1 is the lesson of diminishing returns. Causes 5, 6, 7, and 8 account for about 9 percent of the variation in the process outcomes. Assuming that it will cost about the same to control the second set of four causes as it costs to control the first four causes, the payback for controlling Causes 5, 6, 7, and 8 is about one-tenth as great as that for controlling Causes 1, 2, 3, and 4. Thus, the first four causes of Figure 3.1 are known as the *critical few* cause-and-effect relationships.

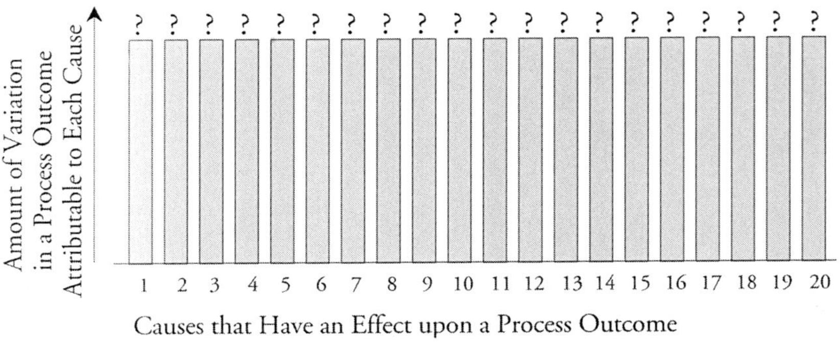

Figure 3.2: What We Usually Know About Causes and Effects

Clearly, when setting up a production process, the objective is to identify and control the critical few cause-and-effect relationships for each of the key process outcomes. The only problem is that Figure 3.1 requires perfect knowledge. In the absence of such knowledge, what can we do?

We generally start off as shown in Figure 3.2, and ask R&D to sort out the gaps in our knowledge. To do this R&D will need to find the amount of variation attributable to each Cause. Next they will need to identify the critical few causes, and for each of these they will need to establish the appropriate levels to be used in production.

Unfortunately, due to pressures of time and money, it is a rare thing for R&D to ever study all of the causes on the list. Generally they will use both theory and experience to choose which causes to study. The rest of the causes on the list will simply be ignored, or perhaps, held constant.

Figure 3.3 shows the causes studied by R&D for their impact upon Product Characteristic Number 2. While they had a list of twenty causes, they only had time to study what they thought were the top ten. Among these ten they found Causes 5, 1, and 7 to be the dominant factors, with Cause 4 trailing along behind. Thus they told

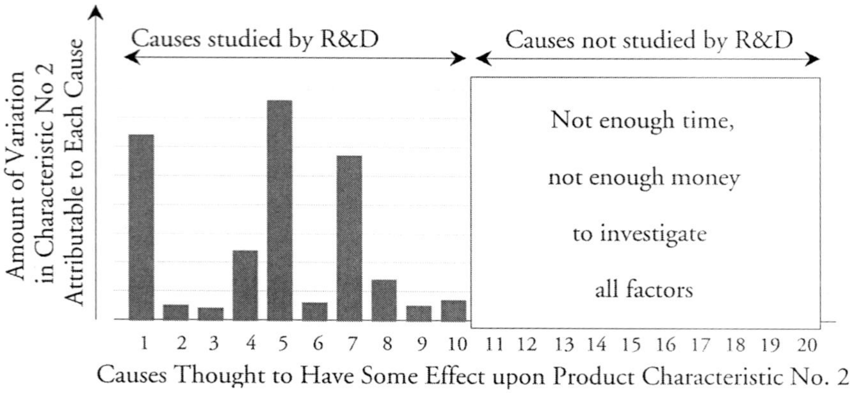

Figure 3.3: Causes Studied by R&D for Characteristic No. 2

the Production Department that they needed to control Causes 5, 1, and 7.

So the production process was set up using Causes 5, 1, and 7 as Control Factors for Product Characteristic No. 2. However, at the start of production they immediately had problems with too much variation in Product Characteristic No. 2 which resulted in a high scrap rate. So they decided to add Cause 4 to the set of Control Factors. It didn't help. As they fell further and further behind the production schedule, and as the mountain of scrap increased, they began to talk about the "skill" that it took to make this product. Words like "art" and "magic" were used. Inspection and rework facilities were expanded, and soon the production department had settled down to the routine that is all too common in production—"burn the toast and scrape it."

Of course, the problem was not with the set of Control Factors—by virtue of their being controlled these causes ceased to be sources of variation for the product stream. Likewise the problem was not with the other six causes studied by R&D—these causes all had small

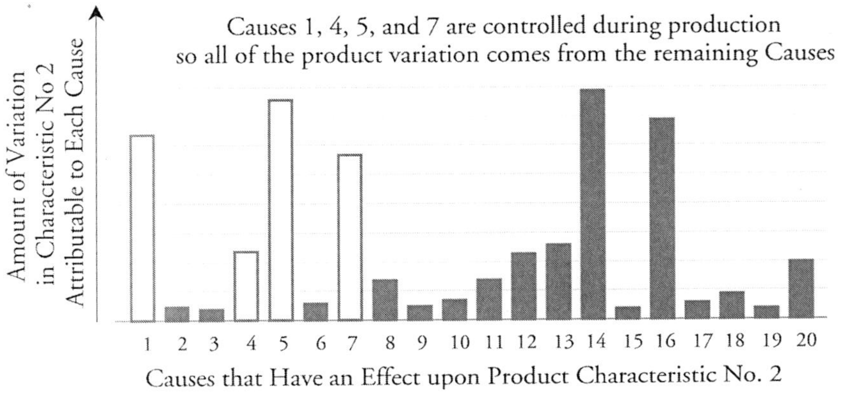

Figure 3.4: Causes That Affect Characteristic No. 2

effects upon Characteristic No. 2. No, the problem was with the factors not studied in R&D. As seen in Figure 3.4, Causes 14 and 16 are dominant cause-and-effect relationships for Product Characteristic No. 2. They are as big, or bigger than Causes 5, 1, and 7. But they were not studied.

Although the manufacturer was not aware of the impact of Causes 14 and 16, the process continued to be under their influence. Since Causes 14 and 16 had not been studied, and were *thought* to be part of the lesser causes, the manufacturer was not exerting any control over the levels of these two factors. Yet, in the course of events, when the levels of either one of these causes changed it would result in a corresponding change in the product characteristic. While the manufacturer remained unaware of impact of Causes 14 and 16, he suffered the consequences of their effects.

So, for any product characteristic, the set of dominant cause-and-effect relationships which the manufacturer chooses to control will constitute the set of Control Factors. All remaining cause-and-effect relationships will belong to the set of Uncontrolled Factors.

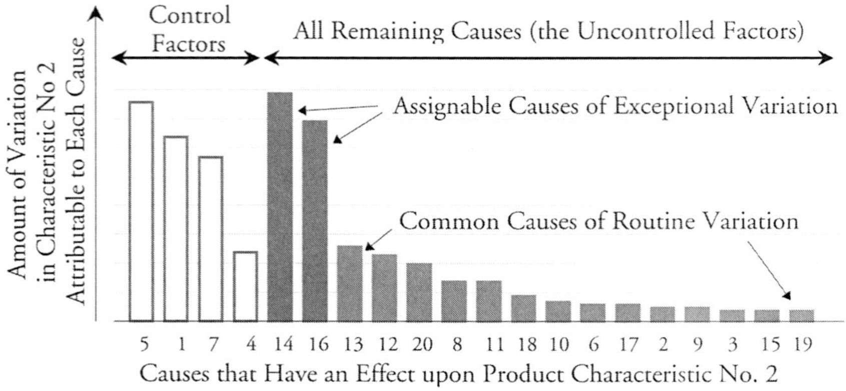

Figure 3.5: Three Types of Cause-and-Effect Relationships

Whenever this latter group contains a dominant cause-and-effect relationship, this dominant uncontrolled cause will haunt the process, creating exceptional variation, excess costs, and general grief.

These dominant but uncontrolled causes were called "Assignable Causes" by Shewhart and "Special Causes" by Deming. (The remaining, lesser, uncontrolled causes were called "Common Causes" by Deming and "Chance Causes" by Shewhart.)

Thus, we have Control Factors, Assignable Causes, and Common Causes. Since the levels of the Control Factors are fixed, they contribute little or no variation to the product characteristic. When we place a factor in the control group, we essentially remove it as a source of process variation. This is why *effort spent trying to fine tune the Control Factors will be of marginal benefit as long as there are Assignable Causes present.* It does not matter what levels of Factors 5, 1, and 7 we choose to use as long as we are doing nothing about Factors 14 and 16!

You cannot optimize any system when some of the dominant cause-and-effect relationships remain unidentified.

HIGH AND LOW PAYBACK STRATEGIES

Since the group of Assignable Causes will contain *all* of those dominant factors that are not in the set of Control Factors, this group will be the source of *most* of the unexplained variation in the product. This is the group of factors that is the major contributor to excess costs of production, low quality, scrap, and rework. Therefore, effort spent in identifying Assignable Causes, and making them part of the group of Control Factors, will generally have a very high payback.

Finally the group of Common Causes will be the source of the run-of-the-mill, routine variation that is always part of the background of all production processes. Effort spent trying to control the Common Causes will, at best, yield small returns, and will usually be effort wasted.

When the group of Uncontrolled Factors contains nothing but Common Causes the process will have reached an economic equilibrium. The product stream will have the greatest degree of uniformity that is consistent with economic production.

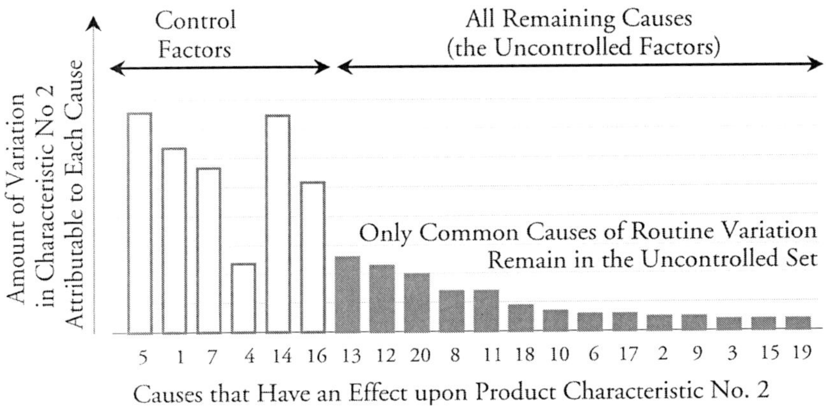

Figure 3.6: The Objective is to Control All Dominant Causes

EXPERIMENTATION IS NOT ENOUGH

It is important to note that whenever we identify a dominant cause-and-effect relationship, and then make that cause a member of the set of Control Factors, we will remove a source of variation from the process. This means that those dominant causes that are discovered in the R&D phase and placed in the set of Control Factors will result in reduced product variation. However, a partial understanding of which factors are dominant will only result in a partial reduction of variation. And every R&D effort is limited by the ability of the researchers to identify the key factors in advance.

Whenever we decide to conduct an experiment there will always be more factors than we can possibly study. Therefore, we will have to choose between those factors that we want to study and those factors that we will have to leave out of the study. These excluded factors may be held constant, or randomized, or ignored, but since they are not studied their impact will remain unknown. Whenever a dominant cause ends up being held constant, or randomized, or ignored, your experiment can only give you a limited and partial understanding of your process.

This means that an experimental approach is limited by the ability of the researchers to identify *all* of the dominant cause-and-effect relationships *prior to doing the experiments.* What is discovered by means of experiments may well be true, but the story may also be incomplete.

However, in spite of our understanding of which factors are dominant, our process will always be subject to the effects of all of the Uncontrolled Factors. When the set of Uncontrolled Factors contains Assignable Causes our process will suffer the consequences.

SUMMARY

This means that you will need to complement any R&D program with a series of Observational Studies to determine if your process contains any "Factors 14 and 16." It is only as you listen to and learn from the process data, that you can develop a complete understanding of your process. Using this understanding you can operate your process more profitably. Without this understanding, you will continue to operate at the mercy of the Assignable Causes.

Therefore, you need to use a technique that will:

- allow you to learn from your process data;
- warn you when your process changes;
- help you to identify the causes of those changes; and
- enable you to operate your process predictably and on target.

Process behavior charts do all of these things. They complement and complete any R&D program, and they provide an essential foundation for any process improvement effort. The alternative to their use is nothing less than chaos.

CHAPTER FOUR

THREE QUESTIONS FOR SUCCESS

Improvement requires a framework. We all need some way to align our efforts and focus on a specific objective. To this end I have found the following questions to be especially helpful.

1. What do you want to accomplish?

Until you have a clearly stated objective, you risk everyone running off in different directions, working on their own pet projects, and not cooperating for the common good. Whether it is a specific project with a limited scope, or the general day-to-day operations of your organization, a clearly stated purpose or objective is important to help focus the thoughts and efforts of everyone involved.

Any situation in which this question remains unanswered will rapidly deteriorate into chaos. However, merely specifying your objective will not be enough.

2. By what method will you accomplish your objective?

While it may be necessary to have a goal, merely having a goal is, by itself, not sufficient. Remember the old saying, "If wishes were horses then beggars would ride." Until you have a plan for achieving your objective, it will be nothing more than a dream.

3. How will you know when you have accomplished your objective?

If you are going to have a goal, and if you hope to move toward that goal, then you will also need some way to measure how far you have come and how far you have yet to go in reaching that goal.

Any measure you might use will vary in the normal course of events. Some months it will go up, and other months it will go down. If you do not know how to determine when a change has occurred, you will have difficulty in separating meaningless changes from a signal that you have made progress toward your goal.

Shewhart discussed these three questions in the context of making a product. He referred to them under the headings of (1) Specifications, (2) Production, and (3) Inspection.

Deming talked about these three questions in terms of (1) having a Criterion, (2) having a Test Method for determining compliance to the criterion, and (3) having a Decision Rule for interpreting the results of the test.

Regardless of the nomenclature, these three questions define the essence of how to get things done. Until we can answer the second and third questions, all of our targets, all of our goals, and all of our plans are merely wishes and hopes. To turn dreams into reality we have to have some specific method for making them come true, and some way to judge when they have come true.

In his second book, *Statistical Method from the Viewpoint of Quality Control,* Shewhart returned to the idea embodied in these three questions and showed how a process behavior chart (1) defines an Ideal, (2) provides a Method, and (3) allows us to make a Judgment.

Specifically, in Figure 4.1 the Natural Process Limits on an *X* Chart define the *process potential.* They define what a predictable process is likely to continue to produce, and they approximate what an unpredictable process can be made to produce if and when it is

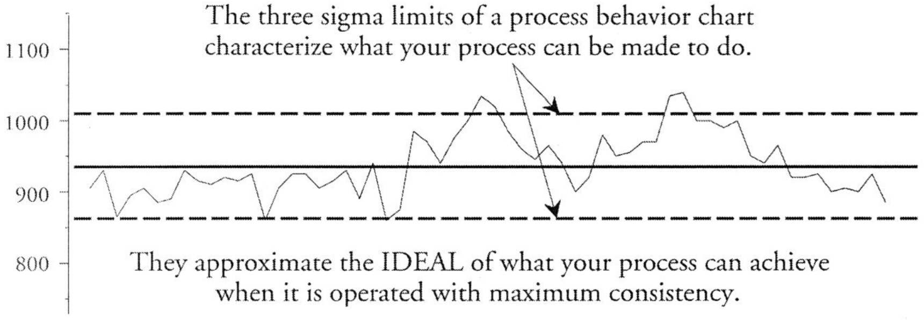

Figure 4.1: What Do You Want to Accomplish?

operated predictably. To use Shewhart's word, the Natural Process Limits define the *Ideal* of what the process can do when it is operated up to its full potential. They define what any process can accomplish.

In Figure 4.2 the running record of the individual values defines the actual *process performance.* Whenever a point goes outside the bounds of the Natural Process Limits it identifies a departure from the routine, a change in the process, and the presence of an Assignable Cause of exceptional variation. By identifying these points the process behavior chart provides us with a methodology for when to look for Assignable Causes. When we can identify an Assignable Cause and move it from the set of Uncontrolled Factors to the set of

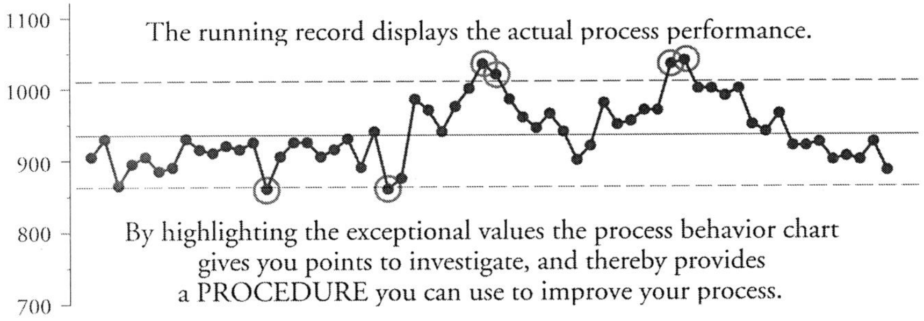

Figure 4.2: By What Method Will You Accomplish It?

Controlled Factors we will be removing a significant source of variation from the product stream. By removing sources of variation from the product stream we are not merely maintaining the status quo, but are rather tightening up on the process variation and improving both the predictability of the process and the consistency of the process outcomes. So the process behavior chart gives us a *Method* for actually moving our process toward the *Ideal.*

Finally, in Figure 4.3, by combining both the process potential and the process performance on the same graph, the process behavior chart allows us to *Judge* how close our process is coming to operating up to its full potential. The absence of points outside the limits tells of a reasonable degree of predictability. For an unpredictable process, the number of points outside the limits and the extent to which they fall outside the limits will quantify the degree of unpredictability.

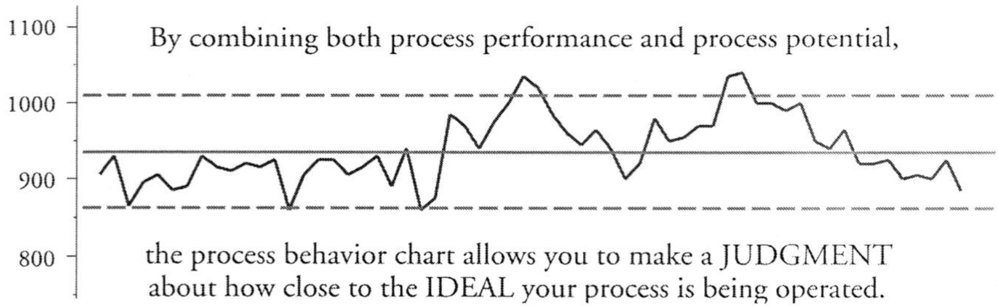

Figure 4.3: How Will You Know When You Have Accomplished It?

SUMMARY

The general framework defined by these three questions is sometimes referred to as an *operational definition.* As may be seen above, the process behavior chart provides us with an operational definition of how to get the most out of any process. It is a definition that you can do business with. Everything else is just wishful thinking.

CHAPTER FIVE

WHERE DO THE SCALING FACTORS COME FROM?

THE SCALING FACTORS FOR THE AVERAGE MOVING RANGE

The primary way to compute limits for an *XmR* Chart depends upon the *Average* and the *Average Moving Range.* The Average of the *k* individual values is taken as the central line for the *X* Chart and the average of the (*k*–1) moving ranges (the Average Moving Range) is taken as the central line for the *mR* Chart. Then limits are computed according to the following:

To find the *Upper and Lower Natural Process Limits* for the *X* Chart
you multiply the *Average Moving Range* by 2.66
and add and subtract the product to and from the *Average.*

$$UNPL = \bar{X} + (2.66 \times \overline{mR})$$

$$LNPL = \bar{X} - (2.66 \times \overline{mR})$$

To find the *Upper Range Limit* for the *mR* Chart:
multiply the *Average Moving Range* by 3.27.

$$URL = 3.27 \times \overline{mR}$$

The values of 2.66 and 3.27 seen in these formulas are the scaling factors needed to convert these summary statistics into estimates of the three-sigma limits for both the set of individual values, X, and the set of moving range values, mR. These scaling factors were created for the convenience of the user at a time when all of the computations were done by hand. How these scaling factors combine the various bias correction factors of Table A.1 in the Appendix to give three-sigma limits is outlined below.

1. The generic form for three-sigma limits for individual values has the form:

$$Average(X) \pm 3\ Sigma(X)$$

When the limits are based upon the Average Moving Range this is:

$$Average(X) \pm 3\ Sigma(X) \quad = \quad \bar{X} \pm 3\ \frac{\overline{mR}}{d_2}$$

For two-point moving ranges the bias correction factor d_2 is 1.128, resulting in:

$$Average(X) \pm 3\ Sigma(X) \quad = \quad \bar{X} \pm 2.660\ \overline{mR}$$

2. In a similar manner, the generic form for the upper three-sigma limit for two-point moving ranges has the form:

$$Average(R) + 3\ Sigma(R) \quad = \quad Average(R) + 3\ d_3\ Sigma(X)$$

When the limits are based upon the Average Moving Range this is:

$$Average(R) + 3\ d_3\ Sigma(X) \quad = \quad \overline{mR} + 3\ d_3\ \frac{\overline{mR}}{d_2}$$

For two-point moving ranges the bias correction factor d_3 is 0.8525, resulting in:

$$Average(R) + 3\ Sigma(R) \quad = \quad \overline{mR} + 2.267\ \overline{mR} \quad = \quad 3.267\ \overline{mR}$$

THE SCALING FACTORS FOR THE MEDIAN MOVING RANGE

An alternate way to compute limits for an *XmR* Chart depends upon the *Average* and the *Median Moving Range.* The Average of the *k* individual values is taken as the central line for the *X* Chart and the median of the (*k*–1) moving ranges (the Median Moving Range) is taken as the central line for the *mR* Chart. Then limits are computed according to the following:

To find the *Upper and Lower Natural Process Limits* for the *X* Chart
you multiply the *Median Moving Range* by 3.14
and add and subtract the product to and from the *Average.*

$$UNPL = \bar{X} + (3.14 \times \widetilde{mR})$$

$$LNPL = \bar{X} - (3.14 \times \widetilde{mR})$$

To find the *Upper Range Limit* for the *mR* Chart:
multiply the *Median Moving Range* by 3.86.

$$URL = 3.86 \times \widetilde{mR}$$

The values of 3.14 and 3.86 seen in these formulas are the scaling factors needed to convert these summary statistics into estimates of the three-sigma limits. How they combine the various bias correction factors to give three-sigma limits is outlined below. Occasionally, when using this alternate computation, the *Median of the Individual Values* may be used in place of the *Average of the Individual Values* in the formulas. Chapter Thirteen discusses when to use the Median Moving Range.

3. When the limits are based upon the Median Moving Range the formula for the limits for individual values becomes:

$$Average(X) \pm 3\ Sigma(X) \quad = \quad \bar{X} \pm 3\ \frac{\widetilde{mR}}{d_4}$$

For two-point moving ranges the bias correction factor d_4 is 0.954, resulting in:

$$Average(X) \pm 3\ Sigma(X) \quad = \quad \bar{X} \pm 3.145\ \widetilde{mR}$$

4. In a similar manner, when the limits are based upon the Median Moving Range the formula for the Upper Range Limit becomes:

$$Average(R) + 3\ Sigma(R) \quad = \quad d_2\ Sigma(X) + 3\ d_3\ Sigma(X)$$

$$= \ [\ d_2 + 3\ d_3\ ]\ \ Sigma(X) \quad = \quad [\ d_2 + 3\ d_3\ ]\ \frac{\widetilde{mR}}{d_4} \quad = \quad 3.863\ \widetilde{mR}$$

Thus, the scaling factors given with the formulas are those values that will convert the raw statistics into three-sigma limits for both the individual values and the moving ranges. The bias correction factors d_2, d_3, and d_4 are practical constants of great generality which have a fine ancestry of highbrow mathematical theorems (and very complicated formulas). (In 1967 Irving Burr found the values for these bias correction factors for 27 different probability models and effectively proved thereby that we can treat them as constants in practice.)

Combining the universal nature of the bias correction factors with the fact that we will always use two-point moving ranges, we end up with simple formulas dependent upon certain fixed scaling factors which will work with virtually any type of data. If this seems rather like a "one size fits all" approach, it is. When characterizing process behavior, this is sufficient. Complications are not required.

CHAPTER SIX

WHY NOT JUST USE THE STANDARD DEVIATION STATISTIC?

The standard deviation statistic, *s*, computed using all of the data, is commonly taught and is available at the push of a button on most calculators today. So why not use this common measure of dispersion to compute the limits on a process behavior chart?

While the global standard deviation statistic provides a descriptive summary for a *homogeneous* data set, it is incorrect to use it when analyzing the data for evidence of a *possible lack of homogeneity.* The problem here lies in the way the global standard deviation statistic is calculated. Whenever any measure of dispersion is computed using all of the data at one time, the aggregation of the data into a single group contains an implicit assumption that the data set is homogeneous. Since the purpose of the process behavior chart is to examine the data for evidence of a lack of homogeneity, it is important to avoid begging the question by our computations. Hence we must avoid any and all global measures of dispersion when computing limits for a process behavior chart. Specifically, when working with individual values, we will always use the localized, short-term variation captured by the two-point moving ranges to compute our limits.

Table 6.1: The Percentage of On-Time Shipments for Dept. 20

	Year One				Year Two				Year Three			
	Total No.	On-Time	%	*mR*	Total No.	On-Time	%	*mR*	Total No.	On-Time	%	*mR*
Jan	191	176	92.1	—	170	155	91.2	0.0	216	198	91.7	0.3
Feb	203	186	91.6	0.5	270	246	91.1	0.1	247	225	91.1	0.6
Mar	220	202	91.8	0.2	167	151	90.4	0.7	230	209	90.9	0.2
Apr	200	183	91.5	0.3	216	196	90.7	0.3	265	239	90.2	0.7
May	236	215	91.1	0.4	227	206	90.7	0.0	184	165	89.7	0.5
Jun	213	194	91.1	0.0	149	136	91.3	0.6	207	188	90.8	1.1
Jul	212	191	90.1	1.0	182	167	91.8	0.5	178	162	91.0	0.2
Aug	241	215	89.2	0.9	224	206	92.0	0.2				
Sep	159	143	89.9	0.7	246	225	91.5	0.5				
Oct	217	197	90.8	0.9	185	170	91.9	0.4				
Nov	181	165	91.2	0.4	261	239	91.6	0.3				
Dec	113	103	91.2	0.0	140	128	91.4	0.2				

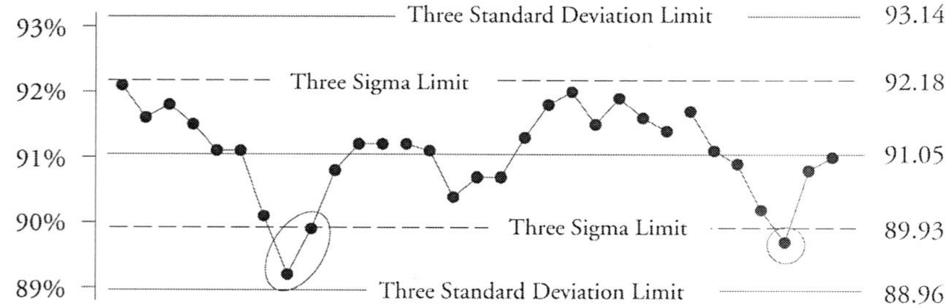

Figure 6.1: Three-Sigma and 3-Standard-Deviation Limits for Table 6.1

To illustrate the importance of computing the limits in the manner shown in the previous chapter we will use the On-Time Shipment data from Department 20 in Table 6.1.

The Average is 91.05, the Average Moving Range is 0.423, and the global standard deviation statistic is $s = 0.697$. Figure 6.1 shows both the three-sigma limits based on the Average Moving Range (dashed lines) and the much wider three-standard-deviation limits (solid lines). While the three-sigma limits show distinct signals of process changes, the three-standard-deviation limits do not detect any signals at all.

Whenever the data contain signals of change these signals will inflate any measure of dispersion that is computed globally. This is why we cannot, under any circumstances, use the global standard deviation statistic to compute limits for a process behavior chart.

BUT WHAT IF THE DATA ARE HOMOGENEOUS?

When the data are reasonably homogeneous the global standard deviation statistic will give limits that are quite similar to those obtained by using the moving ranges. Figure 6.2 shows the *X* Chart for the In-Process Inventory Data from Table 6.2 with both three-sigma limits and three-standard-deviation limits. For Table 6.2 the Average is 20.39, the Average Moving Range is 4.70, and the global standard deviation statistic is 3.81.

The three-standard-deviation limits (solid lines) and the three-

Table 6.2: In-Process Inventory Values for Department 17

(Hundreds of Pounds)

	Jan	Feb	Mar	Apr	May	Jun	Jul	Aug	Sep	Oct	Nov	Dec
Year One	19	27	20	16	18	25	22	24	17	25	15	17
Year Two	20	22	19	16	22	19	25	22	18	20	16	17
Year Three	20	15	27	25	17	19	28					

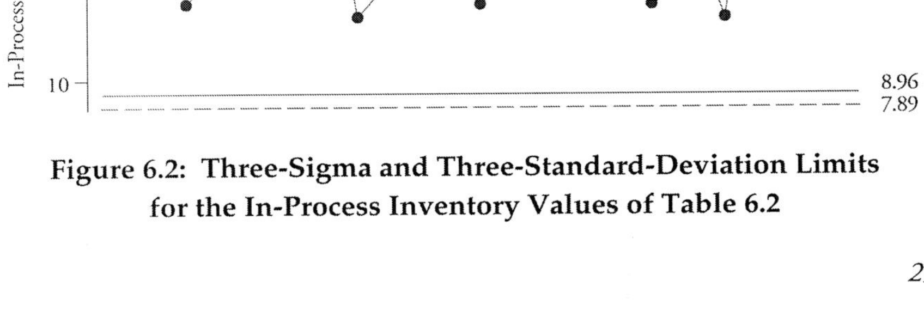

Figure 6.2: Three-Sigma and Three-Standard-Deviation Limits for the In-Process Inventory Values of Table 6.2

sigma limits (dashed lines) tell the same story here. Routine variation can result in monthly values ranging from a low of 8 or 9 up to a high of 31 or 32 while the process averages 20.

This convergence of the two sets of limits that occurs when the data are homogeneous should not be misinterpreted as a justification for using the global standard deviation statistic to compute limits. The global standard deviation statistic has never been, and will never be, the correct way to compute limits for a process behavior chart, as was pointed out by Walter Shewhart on page 302 of his 1931 book, *Economic Control of Quality of Manufactured Product.*

The Average Moving Range and the Median Moving Range constitute the complete list of the practical ways of computing limits for charts for individual values. These two ways provide empirical limits that will reliably separate the routine variation from the exceptional variation as long as the user organizes the data in a rational manner.

COULD WE USE SOME OTHER MEASURE OF DISPERSION ?

When using an *XmR* Chart we will always use two-point moving ranges for the simple reason that two-point moving ranges are both 100 percent efficient and easy to compute. Three-point moving ranges are less efficient and more trouble to compute. Ditto for four-point and all other moving ranges. There is simply no reason to ever use anything other than a two-point moving range with an *XmR* Chart.

But what about using a two-point moving standard deviation statistic? When there are only two data points available to compute a measure of dispersion, the standard deviation statistic will always be equal to the range statistic divided by the square root of 2:

$$s = \frac{R}{\sqrt{2}} \qquad \text{(only when } n = 2\text{)}$$

This means that the two-point moving ranges will contain exactly the same information as the two-point moving standard deviation statistics. Moreover, by avoiding the division by the square root of 2, the two-point moving ranges will be much easier to work with. Hence, once more, there is no reason to ever use anything other than two-point moving ranges when working with charts for individual values.

SOFTWARE ISSUES

Thus, there are right and wrong ways of computing limits for process behavior charts. This is not a matter of opinion, but a statement of a mathematical fact. Chapter Five and Appendix Tables A.2, A.3, and A.4 give the correct formulas for the commonly used charts.

Unfortunately, virtually every software program gives you the option of computing the limits incorrectly. This means that you will need to verify any computational option you wish to use to make sure it computes the limits correctly.

As these examples illustrate, the correct and incorrect ways of computing limits will yield substantially different limits only when the data display a lack of homogeneity. Therefore, when verifying the computations of any software package you should use a data set that contains signals of change. If the software gives limits that do not agree with the limits computed using the formulas and scaling factors from recognized tables, then it is wrong.

When you use an incorrect method of computing limits you can be classified as being either ignorant or dishonest. After reading this chapter you can no longer claim the excuse of ignorance.

CHAPTER SEVEN

DON'T WE NEED NORMAL DATA?

No, we don't.

Three-sigma limits are sufficiently general to work with all kinds of data. Remember, the objective is to separate the routine variation from the exceptional variation. Since the exceptional variation is, by definition, dominant, we only need to filter out the bulk of the routine variation in order to tell the difference. Thus, we need limits that will cover all, or almost all, of the routine variation.

To see how three-sigma limits do this, we can use various probability models to characterize routine variation. Figure 7.1 contains six such models ranging from the uniform distribution to the exponential distribution. Each of these models was standardized so that they all have a mean of zero and a standard deviation parameter of 1.00. Figure 7.1 shows the three-sigma limits and that proportion of the area under each curve that falls within those three-sigma limits.

There are four lessons that can be learned from Figure 7.1.

The first lesson of Figure 7.1 is that three-sigma limits will filter out virtually all of the routine variation regardless of the shape of the histogram. These six models are radically different, yet in spite of these differences, three-sigma limits cover 98 percent to 100 percent of the area under each curve.

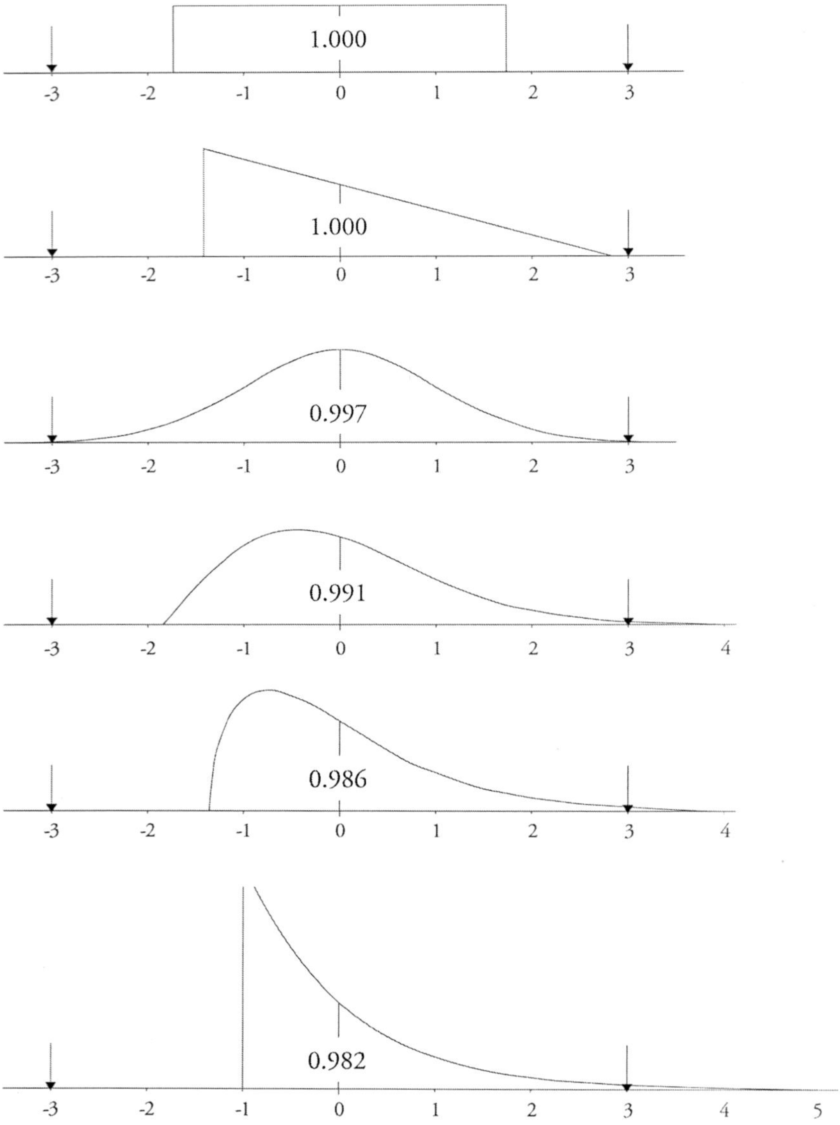

Figure 7.1: How Three-Sigma Limits Filter Out Virtually All of the Routine Variation Regardless of the Probability Model Used

The second lesson of Figure 7.1 is that any data point that falls outside the three-sigma limits is a potential signal of a process change. Since it will be a rare event for routine variation to take you outside the three-sigma limits, it is more likely that any point that falls outside these limits is a signal of a process change.

The third lesson of Figure 7.1 is that symmetric, three-sigma limits work with skewed data. Four of the six models shown are skewed. As we scan down the page we see that no matter how skewed the model becomes, the standard deviation parameter is stretched at essentially the same rate as the tail. This means that the length of the elongated tail will effectively determine the three-sigma distance in each case, and that the limits will cover the bulk of the elongated tail no matter how skewed the data become.

"But that certainly makes the other limit look silly." Yes, it does. Here we need to pause and think about those situations where we have skewed data. In most cases we have skewed data when the data pile up against a barrier or boundary condition. Whenever a boundary value falls within the computed limits, the boundary takes precedence over the computed limit, and we end up with a one-sided chart. When this happens the remaining limit covers the long tail and allows us to separate the routine variation from potential signals of deviation away from the boundary. Hence, symmetric, three-sigma limits work with skewed data.

The fourth lesson of Figure 7.1 is that any uncertainty in where we draw the three-sigma lines will not greatly affect the coverage of the limits. All of the curves are so flat by the time they reach the neighborhood of the three-sigma limits that any errors we may make when we estimate the limits will have, at most, a minimal impact upon how the chart works.

The six probability models in Figure 7.1 effectively summarize what was found when this author looked at over 1100 probability models from seven commonly used families of models. These 1143 models effectively covered all of the shape characterization plane, with 916 mound-shaped models, 182 J-shaped models, and 45 U-shaped models. Eleven hundred and twelve of these models had better than 97.5 percent of their area covered by symmetric three-sigma limits.

Three-sigma limits work by brute force. They are sufficiently general to work with all types and shapes of histograms. They work with skewed data, and they work even when our estimates are based on few data.

Therefore, we do not have to pre-qualify our data before we place them on a process behavior chart. We do not need to define a reference distribution prior to computing limits. Neither do we need to transform our data before we place them on a process behavior chart.

Anyone who tells you anything to the contrary is simply trying to complicate your life unnecessarily.

CHAPTER EIGHT

BUT THE SOFTWARE TRANSFORMS THE DATA!

The first principle for understanding data is that no data have meaning apart from their context. Analysis begins with context, is driven by context, and ends with the results being interpreted in the context of the original data. This principle requires that there must always be a link between what you do with the data and the original context for the data. Any transformation of the data risks breaking this linkage.

If a transformation makes sense both in terms of the original data and the objectives of the analysis, then it will be okay to use that transformation. Transformations of this type might be things like the use of daily or weekly averages in place of hourly values, or the use of proportions or rates in place of counts to take into account the differing areas of opportunity in different time periods.

Only you as the user can determine when a transformation will make sense in the context of the data. (The software cannot do this because it will never know the context.) Moreover, since these sensible transformations will tend to be fairly simple in nature, they do not tend to distort the data.

A second class of transformations would be those that rescale the data in order to achieve certain statistical properties. (These are the only type of transformations that any software can suggest.) Here the objective is usually to make the data appear to be more "normally distributed" in order to have an "estimate of dispersion that is independent of the estimate of location." Unfortunately, these transformations will tend to be very complex and nonlinear in nature, involving exponential, inverse exponential, or logarithmic functions. (And just what does the logarithm of the percentage of on-time shipments represent?) These nonlinear transformations will distort the data in two ways: at one end of the histogram, values that were originally far apart will now be close together; at the other end of the histogram, values that were originally close together will now be far apart.

To illustrate the effect of transformations to achieve statistical properties we will use the Hot Metal Transit Times shown in rows in Table 8.1. These values are the times (to the nearest five minutes) between the phone call alerting the steel furnace that a load of hot metal was on the way and the actual arrival of that load at the steel furnace ladle house. The histogram is shown in Figure 8.1.

Given the skewed nature of these data some programs would suggest using a logarithmic transformation. Taking the natural logarithm of each of these transit times results in the histogram in Figure 8.2. (The horizontal scales show both the original and transformed values.) Notice how the values on the left of Figure 8.2 are spaced out while those on the right are crowded together. After the transformation the distance from 20 to 25 minutes is about the same size as the distance from 140 to 180 minutes. How could you begin to explain this to your boss?

By itself, this distortion of the data is sufficient to call into question the practice of transforming the data to achieve statistical properties. However, the impact of these non-linear transformations is not confined to the histograms.

Table 8.1: The Hot Metal Transit Times in Minutes

40	45	125	100	40	40	100	65	55	40	125	65	40	45	95
105	45	110	40	50	120	45	65	105	35	70	55	25	50	55
50	40	40	45	55	50	45	125	55	100	40	70	40	40	110
55	50	30	50	105	45	45	55	50	25	65	60	60	55	70
55	45	100	60	45	145	45	50	65	180	60	45	35	35	55
55	55	50	120	35	45	35	45	55	50	70	45	75	60	45
60	40	60	40	50	60	65	95	65	60	50	25	25	100	50
60	45	35	40	30	180	50	30	30	30	65	130	80	20	45
65	65	45	40	50	25	120	30	115	50	85	40	35	40	40
55	50	25	75	55	50									

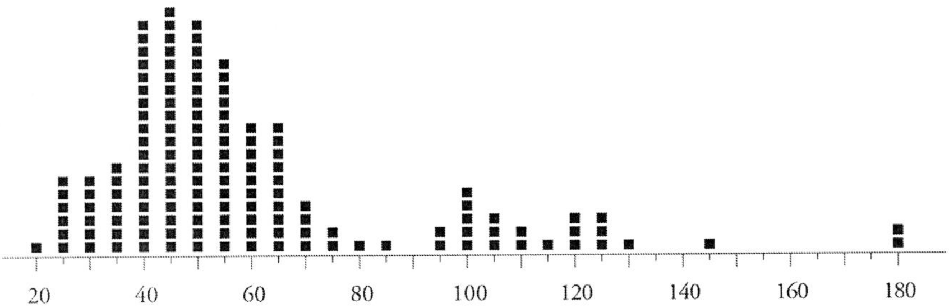

Figure 8.1: Histogram of the Hot Metal Transit Times

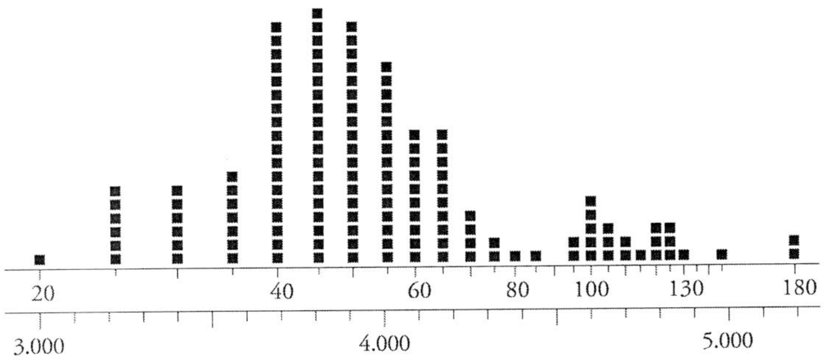

Figure 8.2: Histogram of the Logarithms of Hot Metal Transit Times

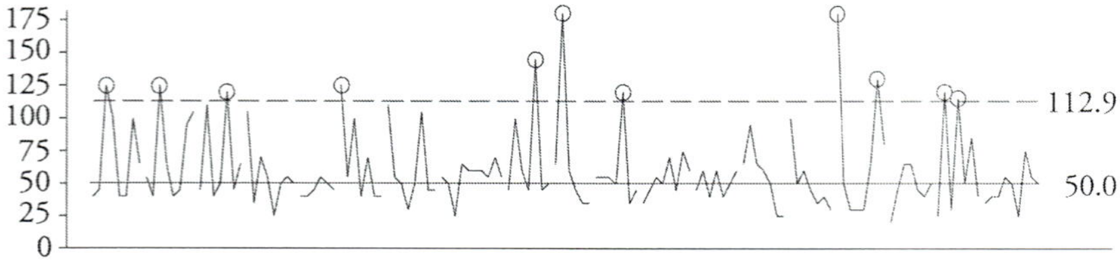

Figure 8.3: *X* Chart for the Hot Metal Transit Times

Figure 8.3 shows the *X* Chart for the original, untransformed data of Table 8.1. Eleven of the 141 transit times are above the upper limit, confirming the impression given by the histogram that these data come from a mixture of at least two different processes. Even after the steel furnace gets the phone call, they still have no idea when the hot metal will arrive at the ladle house.

However, if we transform the data before we put them on a process behavior chart we end up with Figure 8.4. There we find no points outside the limits!

Clearly the logarithmic transformation has obliterated the signals. What good is a transformation that changes the message contained within the data? The transformation of the data to achieve statistical properties is simply a complex way of distorting both the data and the truth.

The results shown here are typical of what happens with nonlinear

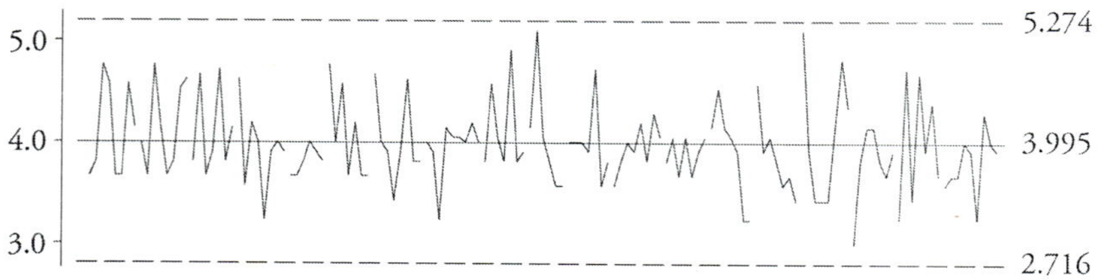

Figure 8.4: *X* Chart for the Logarithms of the Hot Metal Transit Times

transformations of the original data. These transformations hide the signals contained within the data simply because they are based upon computations that *presume there are no signals within the data.*

To see how the computations do this we need to pause to consider the nature of the formulas for common descriptive statistics. For a descriptive measure of location we usually use the average, which is simply based upon the sum of the data. However, once we leave the average behind the formulas become much more complex. For a descriptive measure of dispersion we commonly use the global standard deviation statistic, which is a function of the *squared deviations from the average.* For descriptive measures of shape we commonly use the skewness and kurtosis statistics which, respectively, depend upon the *third* and *fourth* powers of the deviations of the data from the average. When we aggregate the data together in this manner and use the second, third, and fourth powers of the distance between each observation and the average value, we are implicitly assuming that these computations make sense. Whether they be measures of dispersion, or measures of skewness, or even measures of kurtosis, *any high-order descriptive statistic that is computed globally is implicitly based upon a very strong assumption that the data are homogeneous.*

When the data are not homogeneous it is not the *shape* of the histogram that is wrong, but the computation and use of the descriptive statistics that is erroneous. We do not need to distort the histogram to make the transformed values more homogeneous, but we need to stop and question what the lack of homogeneity means in the context of the original observations.

So how can we determine when a data set is homogeneous? That is the purpose of the process behavior chart! Transforming the data to achieve statistical properties prior to placing them on a process behavior chart is an example of getting everything backwards. It assumes that we need to make the data more homogeneous prior to checking them for homogeneity. Any recommendation regarding the transformation of the data prior to placing them on a chart reveals a fundamental lack of understanding about the purpose of the process behavior chart technique.

Shewhart's approach, with its generic limits computed empirically from the data, does not even require the specification of a probability model. In fact, on page 54 of *Statistical Method from the Viewpoint of Quality Control*, Shewhart wrote "*...we are not concerned with the functional form of the universe* [i.e., the probability model], *but merely with the assumption that a universe exists."* [Italics in the original.]

When you transform the data to achieve statistical properties you deceive both yourself and everyone else who is not sophisticated enough to catch you in your deception.

Beware of computations that triumph over common sense!

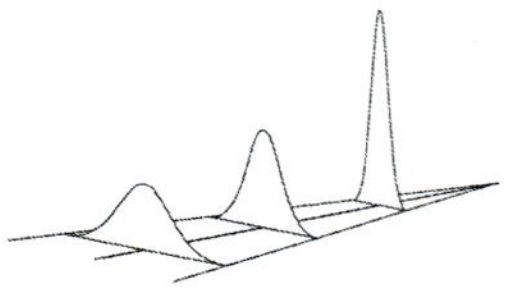

CHAPTER NINE

WHY USE THREE-SIGMA LIMITS?

The two technical foundations of process behavior charts are the use of the within-subgroup variation and the use of three-sigma limits. The conceptual foundation is the notion of rational subgrouping. In Chapters Five and Six the use of within-subgroup variation was shown to be the only correct way of computing the limits. In Chapters Seven and Eight we learned a little about how three-sigma limits work. But why did Shewhart choose three-sigma limits instead of some other multiple of sigma?

As we saw in Figure 7.1, three-sigma limits work with all types of data. They will filter out virtually all of the routine variation, so that anything left over can be considered to be a potential signal of exceptional variation. And three-sigma limits are reasonably conservative, so that we do not have to wait until we have a lot of data before we can compute useful limits. In Shewhart's own words:

> "Hence we must use limits such that through their use we will not waste too much time looking unnecessarily for trouble."
>
> "The method of attack is to establish limits of variability... such that, when [an observation] is found outside these limits, looking for an assignable cause is worth while [*sic*]."

> "If more than one statistic is used, then the limits ... should be chosen so that the probability of looking for trouble ... is economic."
>
> "... we usually choose a symmetrical range characterized by limits..."
>
> *Average* ± *t Sigma*
>
> "Experience indicates that $t = 3$ seems to be an acceptable economic value."
>
> "Hence the method for establishing allowable limits of variation in a statistic ... depends upon theory to furnish [the estimates] and upon empirical evidence to justify the choice of limits..."
>
> *Average* ± 3 *Sigma*

Thus three-sigma limits are the result of a blend of mathematical theory and empirical evidence. They have been thoroughly proven in practice. Yet British Standard 600 suggests using 3.09 sigma limits, and many software packages allow you to choose something other than three-sigma limits. So why should we use three-sigma limits today?

If you truly want an answer to this question you need to study pages 148 to 302 of Shewhart's *Economic Control of Quality of Manufactured Product.* The quotations above come from this 155 page argument that Shewhart used to support his choice of three-sigma limits. As Shewhart noted, when the computations are built on mathematical theory, they do not go out of style. The Pythagorean Theorem, Pascal's Triangle, and Laplace's Central Limit Theorem are still in use today. What worked for Shewhart will still work for you.

In my experience, most recommendations for the use of something other than three-sigma limits are based upon a misunderstanding of the distinction between Experimental Studies and Observational Studies.

In an Experimental Study, where there is a fixed amount of data and where we want to use the most precise analysis possible, the argument usually goes something like the following:

Choose some risk of a false alarm,
then, using the appropriate probability model,
find the *exact* critical values that correspond to that risk,
and then use these critical values in your analysis.

Because we only get one chance to analyze data from an Experimental Study, and because we expect our experimental data to contain signals, we will often increase our risk of a false alarm in order to increase the sensitivity of our analysis. (This would correspond to tightening the limits on a process behavior chart.) Here the emphasis is upon extracting all of the information that we can from the limited, and relatively expensive, experimental data.

However, with an Observational Study the analysis is sequential. This means that a new act of analysis is performed every time a new point is added to the chart. Hence, *Shewhart's approach was just the opposite of the traditional approach above.* Rather than starting with the risk of a false alarm, he began with the critical values:

Choose some generic critical values for which
the risk of a false alarm will be reasonably small
regardless of the probability model used,
and use these generic critical values in your analysis.

Three-sigma limits are Shewhart's generic solution to the problem of how to analyze a stream of data from an Observational Study. As shown in Figure 7.1 and in other studies, three-sigma limits are sufficiently conservative to work with virtually all kinds of data.

In practice, with a sequential procedure, we do not really care what the risk of a false alarm turns out to be. As long as the risk remains reasonably small we can make our decision and take appropriate action. However, when people are accustomed to the analysis of experimental data, they will be prone to want to tweak the three-sigma limits in accordance with their own personal preferences regarding the risk of a false alarm.

BUT WOULDN'T TWO-SIGMA LIMITS BE MORE SENSITIVE?

Occasionally the use of two-sigma limits will be suggested. In my experience this suggestion usually occurs after someone has used the global standard deviation statistic to incorrectly compute the limits for a process behavior chart. When the three standard deviation limits turn out to be excessively wide the student is tempted to trim them down a bit by using 2 s instead of 3 s. This amounts to trying to correct one mistake by making another mistake. Unfortunately, two wrongs still do not make one right.

At other times the use of two-sigma limits (correctly computed) is suggested as a way to "make the charts more sensitive." While this may seem like a good idea, it fails to take into account the sequential nature of the process behavior chart technique. Because of this sequential nature, the use of two-sigma limits will simply increase the false alarm rate to the point that the user will lose all credibility. This has been clearly shown and documented in the journals.

Three-sigma limits have a fine ancestry of high-brow statistical theorems, and they have also been thoroughly proven in practice. Do not try to reinvent the wheel. Accept no substitutes. Use the original. So if a stranger, or your software, or even a friend suggests using something other than correctly computed three-sigma limits, just say no!

CHAPTER TEN

HOW MANY DATA DO I NEED FOR LIMITS?

What happens when we use only a few values to create an *XmR* Chart? Specifically, what happens to the likelihood of a false alarm, and what happens to the ability of the chart to detect signals of process changes? Answers to these questions will provide an answer to the question of how many data are needed for computing limits.

THE LIKELIHOOD OF A FALSE ALARM WITHIN THE BASELINE

Mathematical theory tells us that whenever we place a point on an *X* Chart the *average* risk of a false alarm is approximately 0.27%. But what happens to this risk when an *XmR* Chart has only *k* values? Simulation studies by Dr. Henry R. Neave provide the answers shown in Table 10.1 and plotted in Figure 10.1.

Table 10.1: The Effective Average Risk of a False Alarm During the Baseline Period on an *X* Chart

Limits based on an Average Moving Range				Limits based on a Median Moving Range			
k	*Avg. Risk*	*k*	*Avg. Risk*	*k*	*Avg. Risk*	*k*	*Avg. Risk*
4	0	14	0.0024	4	.0268	14	.0109
5	0.0009	15	0.0024	5	.0114	15	.0092
6	0.0021	16	0.0025	6	.0209	16	.0099
7	0.0022	17	0.0025	7	.0126	17	.0086
8	0.0021	18	0.0025	8	.0168	18	.0091
9	0.0022	19	0.0025	9	.0118	19	.0081
10	0.0022	20	0.0025	10	.0141	20	.0085
11	0.0023	25	0.0025	11	.0108	25	.0070
12	0.0023	30	0.0026	12	.0123	30	.0066
13	0.0024	40	0.0026	13	.0100	40	.0056
		100	0.0027			100	.0039

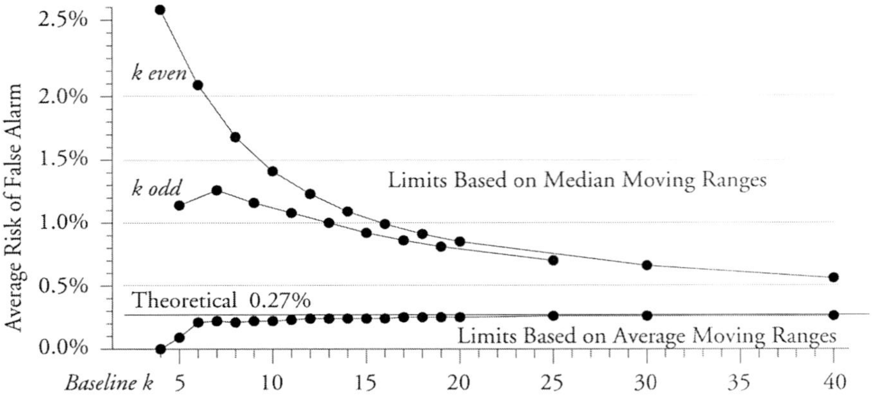

Figure 10.1: The Average Risks of a False Alarm During the Baseline Period

The bottom curve in Figure 10.1 shows the effective average risks of a false alarm for limits based on the Average Moving Range. These risks rapidly approach the theoretical value and then plateau.

The two upper curves in Figure 10.1 are for limits based on a Median Moving Range. Both curves show that the effective average risk of a false alarm drops down toward the theoretical value as the value of *k* increases. Moreover, since risks in the neighborhood of 2.0% are commonly considered to be conservative, we see that the charts maintain their conservative nature even when used with few data.

Thus, when we create a chart using only a few values we will have a reasonably small chance of getting a false alarm within our baseline period. But what about our ability to detect a real signal within the baseline values?

DETECTING A SIGNAL WITHIN THE BASELINE PERIOD

When the baseline data contain values that occur both before and after a change in process location, it is inevitable that the change in location will influence the limits.

When the baseline period contains a large number of values, the effect of any shift that occurs within the baseline period will be diluted. However, when the baseline period contains few data, any shift will have a pronounced impact upon the limits. Thus, it is inevitable that the X Chart will become less able to detect a shift in location that occurs within the baseline period as fewer data are used in the baseline period.

In order to understand the following argument it will be helpful to know that when a shift occurs *following* the baseline period the size of the shift will affect the likelihood of detecting that shift. In fact, as may be seen in Figure 10.2, following the baseline period, a three-sigma shift will generally have a 50-50 chance of being detected on the first observation following the shift.

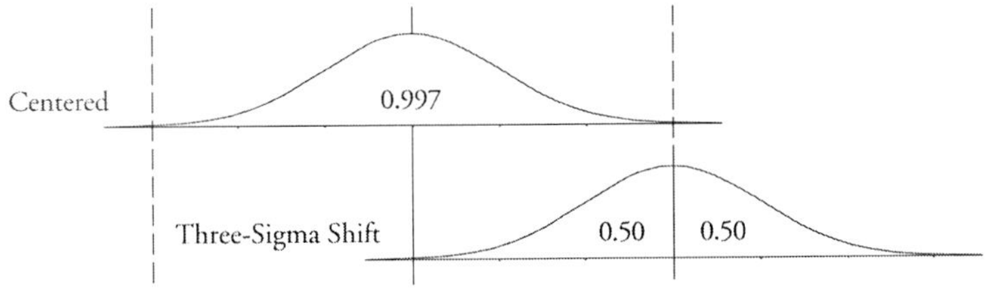

Figure 10.2: A Three-Sigma Shift Has a 50-50 Chance of Detection

To determine how signals within the baseline period affect the sensitivity of the chart, we shall consider how large a shift will need to be in order to be detected half the time. For purposes of the comparisons being made here, I chose a specific type of change where the last value, out of k values, was shifted by some known amount. (Other types of signals might have greater or lesser impacts upon the computed limits, but this signal will be sufficient for our purposes.) For different numbers of baseline values, k, the smallest shift that was

Table 10.2: The Size of Shifts in Sigma Units Occurring on the Last Point Within the Baseline Period That Were Detected Half the Time with *X* Charts Based on *k* Data

Limits based on an Average Moving Range						Limits based on a Median Moving Range					
k	*shift*	*k*	*shift*	*k*	*shift*	*k*	*shift*	*k*	*shift*	*k*	*shift*
4	∞	11	4.18	18	3.53	4	5.95	11	3.85	18	3.42
5	15.23	12	3.99	19	3.54	5	5.32	12	3.69	19	3.45
6	7.55	13	3.89	20	3.47	6	4.77	13	3.69	20	3.37
7	5.83	14	3.78	25	3.37	7	4.49	14	3.61	25	3.31
8	5.03	15	3.73	30	3.29	8	4.12	15	3.58	30	3.26
9	4.59	16	3.68	40	3.22	9	4.01	16	3.53	40	3.20
10	4.33	17	3.62	100	3.07	10	3.88	17	3.49	100	3.07

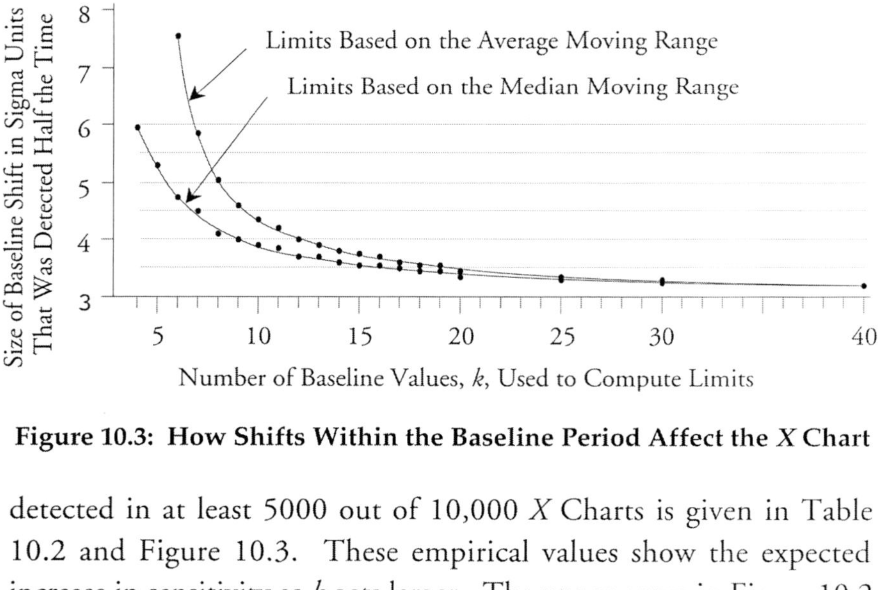

Figure 10.3: How Shifts Within the Baseline Period Affect the *X* Chart

detected in at least 5000 out of 10,000 *X* Charts is given in Table 10.2 and Figure 10.3. These empirical values show the expected increase in sensitivity as *k* gets larger. The upper curve in Figure 10.2 shows what happens when the limits are based on the Average Moving Range. There we see that when *k* is 12 or smaller, the shifts have to exceed 4.0 sigma to be detected half the time.

The lower curve in Figure 10.2 shows what happens when the limits are based on the Median Moving Range. Here we see that these limits display a greater ability to detect changes within the baseline period for small values of *k* than do limits based on the Average Moving Range. However, when *k* is less than 9, even these limits require shifts to exceed 4.0 sigma before they are detected half the time.

These losses of sensitivity suggest that you should exercise reasonable care when choosing a baseline period to make sure that it is free from known changes. While this is good advice for any value of *k*, it is imperative with short baseline periods.

Thus, combining the results from Tables 10.1 and 10.2, we can see that we may construct an XmR Chart using very few data indeed. In the absence of any signals, there will be a reasonably small chance of getting a false alarm. In the presence of actual signals, the limits will be inflated so that any signal we detect will be larger than it looks. All of this means that when you get a point outside the limits within the baseline period you can safely interpret that point as a signal regardless of how few data have been used in constructing the limits.

While you do run the risk of missing some smaller signals by constructing charts using few data, *not* computing the limits and waiting for more data will guarantee that you miss *all* of the signals. Thus, there is no real penalty attached to using a small number of data to compute your initial limits for a process behavior chart.

USING THE LIMITS WITH FUTURE VALUES

In the next chapter the questions surrounding the judgment call on when to revise the limits will be considered. Here I will look at the risks involved in choosing *not* to revise the limits as additional data become available.

If you have computed limits using *k* values and your baseline period shows signals of exceptional variation, then you do not need to worry about revising the limits. Instead, you need to find the assignable cause of the exceptional variation and take action to remove its effect from your process. Revising the limits is moot. Action is required. Following this action you will essentially have a new process and will therefore need to get a new baseline and compute new limits.

If you have limits based on *k* values and your baseline period shows no signals of exceptional variation, then what happens if you choose to use these limits with future values as they become available? Here we will look at what happens to the risks of a false alarm and what happens to the ability of the chart to detect process changes.

Once again we turn to a simulation study by Dr. Henry Neave to get the average risks of a false alarm when limits based on *k* values are used with future observations. As outlined above, these risks apply only when the baseline period contains no signals. As before, the values are given in Table 10.3 and shown in Figure 10.4.

Table 10.3: The Average Risk of a False Alarm on an *X* Chart When Limits Based on *k* Values Are Used Following the Baseline Period

Limits based on an Average Moving Range				Limits based on a Median Moving Range			
k	*Avg. Risk*	*k*	*Avg. Risk*	*k*	*Avg. Risk*	*k*	*Avg. Risk*
4	0.0765	14	0.0144	4	.0663	14	.0146
5	0.0563	15	0.0134	5	.0465	15	.0134
6	0.0428	16	0.0124	6	.0395	16	.0127
7	0.0346	17	0.0117	7	.0314	17	.0118
8	0.0290	18	0.0110	8	.0277	18	.0112
9	0.0249	19	0.0104	9	.0234	19	.0105
10	0.0217	20	0.0098	10	.0213	20	.0101
11	0.0193	25	0.0080	11	.0186	25	.0082
12	0.0173	30	0.0068	12	.0173	30	.0070
13	0.0157	40	0.0055	13	.0155	40	.0056
		100	0.0035			100	.0033

These average risks drop below 2% when *k* is 11 and they drop below 1% when *k* is 20. With limits based on fewer than *k* = 10 data you will be more interested in using additional data to update your limits, subject to the caveat that you will want to avoid the inclusion of a known change, or a potential change, within your baseline period.

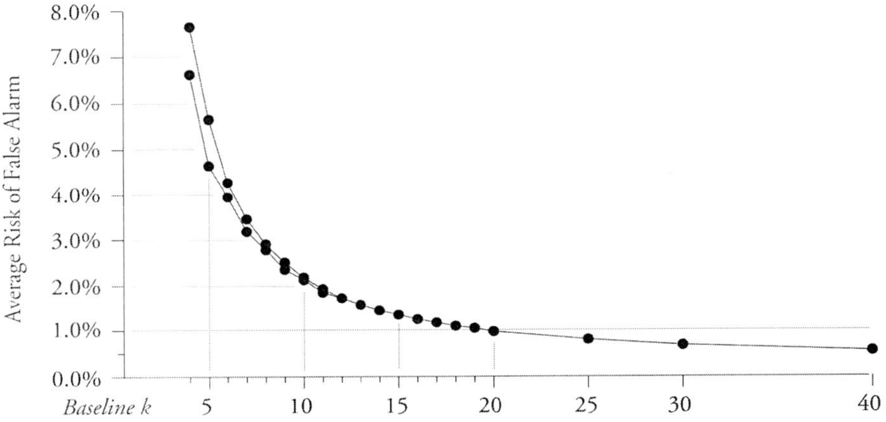

Figure 10.4: The Average Risk of a False Alarm on an *X* Chart Following a Baseline Period Consisting of *k* Values

On the next page Figure 10.5 shows the results of a separate simulation study that characterizes the chances of detecting a three-sigma shift following the baseline period. There we see that limits based on the Average Moving Range are slightly more sensitive than limits based on the Median Moving Range. However, in practice, *all* the departures from the theoretical value shown in Figure 10.5 are too small to have any real impact upon the sensitivity of the chart.

Therefore, using limits from short baselines with future data will expose you to an increased risk of a false alarm, but it will have little effect upon the ability of the X Chart to detect real changes when they occur.

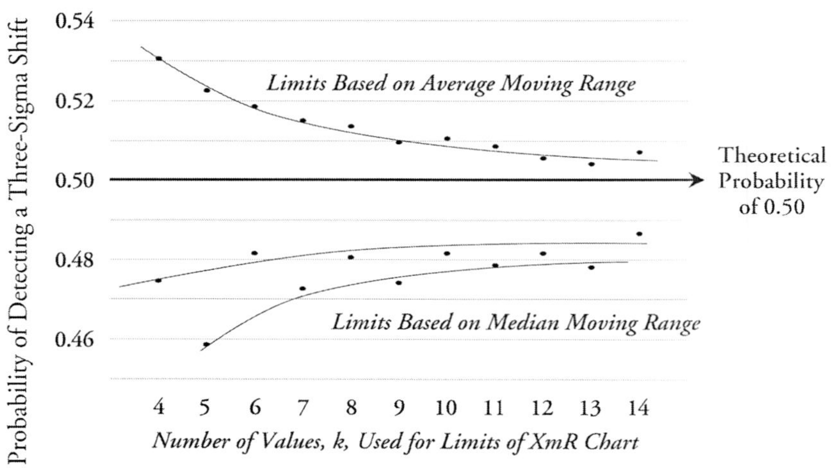

Figure 10.5: How the Number of Baseline Values, *k*, Affects the Likelihood of Detecting a Shift That Occurs After the Baseline Period

SUMMARY

In practice, the number of data used to compute the limits does not have an appreciable impact upon either the false alarm rate within the baseline period or the ability of the charts to detect changes which occur following the baseline period. As long as we exercise reasonable care to avoid known or obvious changes within our baseline period, we can construct an *XmR* Chart using as few as 4 to 6 original data. When additional data become available, we will need to consider if we need to revise the limits to avoid an inflated risk of a false alarm. Issues surrounding this decision are the topic of the next chapter.

Remember, the objective is not to compute the "right" limits, but to use the limits to characterize the behavior of the process. This characterization does not require high precision in our computations, but rather clear thinking about how we use and interpret the data.

CHAPTER ELEVEN

WHEN DO I NEED TO REVISE THE LIMITS?

While we can get good limits from bad data, that is no excuse for knowingly using an inappropriate baseline period. The Fourth Lesson drawn from Figure 7.1 revealed that any uncertainty in where we draw the three-sigma limits will not have an appreciable effect upon the amount of routine variation covered by the limits. Three-sigma limits are so conservative that any errors in estimation will have minimal impact upon how those limits work in practice. Yet, when we know that a given baseline period contains a signal, we may need to modify our baseline period and revise the limits.

Table 11.1: Premium Freight Data

Month Year	Total Number of Shipments	Number Shipped by Air Freight	Percentage Shipped by Air Freight	Moving Ranges
January 01	5858	619	10.57	—
February 01	4084	451	11.04	0.47
March 01	5196	480	9.24	1.80
April 01	4172	450	10.79	1.55
May 01	6144	374	6.09	4.70
June 01	3792	227	5.99	0.10
July 01	4792	278	5.80	0.19
August 01	7226	346	4.79	1.01
September 01	4440	161	3.63	1.16
October 01	4896	232	4.74	1.11
November 01	6019	352	5.85	1.11
December 01	4101	277	6.75	0.90

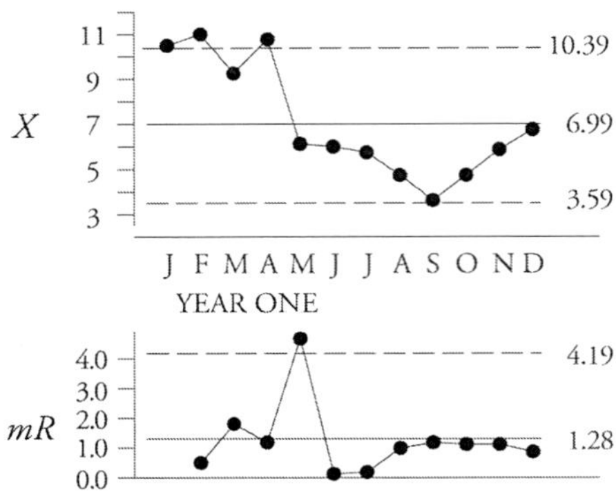

Figure 11.1: *XmR* Chart for Premium Freight Percentages

To illustrate this principle, I will use the Premium Freight Data in Table 11.1. The limits based upon all of the data from Year One are shown in Figure 11.1. After computing these limits, I asked the Transportation Manager about the change indicated in May of Year One. He said, "This was about the time we got all the purchasing agents together in one room and gave them guidelines for when it would be appropriate to use premium freight."

In other words, they had changed the system in May of Year One. Based on this information, we now know that the limits of Figure 11.1 represent neither the old system or the new system. Since the objective is to use the limits to tell the story contained within the data, I decided to compute two sets of limits for Year One. The first set of limits is based on the first four values, while the second set is based on the last eight values. These limits are shown in Figure 11.2.

The first set of limits are of little interest except for comparison with the second set of limits, which presumably represent the current system. Here the requirement of using a rational baseline leads to using fewer values to compute the limits. Now we can use the second set of limits to characterize the new system.

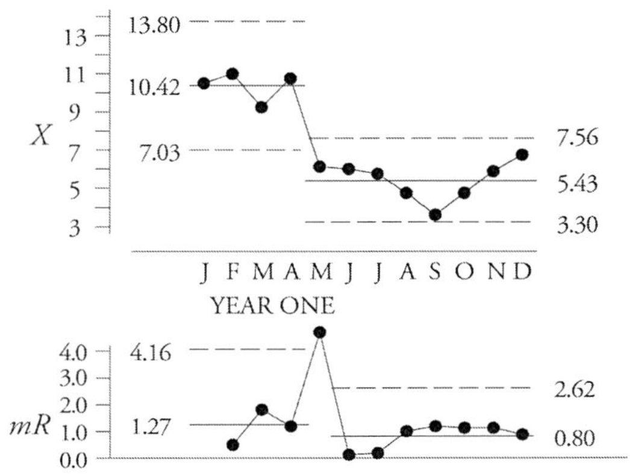

Figure 11.2: Revised *XmR* Chart for Premium Freight Data

So what is the story told by Figure 11.2? In order to reduce freight costs the Transportation Manager has restricted the use of premium freight. In a production system that averages over 5000 incoming shipments each month, they went from having 10.4% shipped in by air to having only 5.4% shipped in by air. This is an average of 253 fewer premium freight shipments each month. What impact do you think this will have on production? What do you think delays in receiving some parts will do to the piles of in-process inventory? But regardless of what happens in the production department, the Transportation Manager will meet his targeted expense reduction!

Here, then, is one more example of making the core process work less efficiently by trying to squeeze the budget of a support group. This is never a good idea. To see what happened here we add the data for Year Two to the chart to get Figure 11.3.

Of course, with additional data available the question of revising the limits will inevitably arise. After all, our limits are only based on eight values! Here we learn more by not revising the limits, but by simply using the existing limits to characterize Year Two.

Table 11.2: Premium Freight Data for Year Two

Month Year	Total No.	No. by Air	Percentage	*mR*
January 02	3775	252	6.68	0.07
February 02	5068	229	4.52	2.16
March 02	4119	252	6.12	1.60
April 02	4075	232	5.69	0.43
May 02	4040	239	5.92	0.23
June 02	4038	274	6.79	0.87
July 02	5275	324	6.14	0.65
August 02	4059	268	6.60	0.46
September 02	5133	361	7.03	0.43
October 02	5311	487	9.17	2.14
November 02	2977	290	9.74	0.57
December 02	5658	506	8.94	0.80

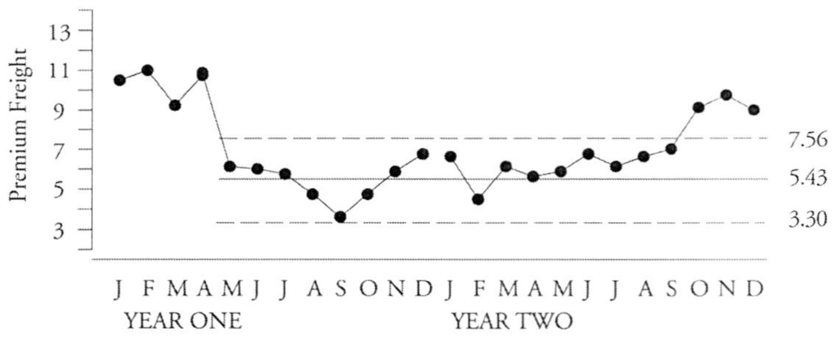

Figure 11.3: *X* Chart for Premium Freight Data for Years One and Two

When the new data are plotted in Figure 11.3 against the limits from Figure 11.2, we can see the pressure from the production department gradually driving up the premium freight percentage until the pressure to meet the production schedule causes a complete breakdown of the guidelines in the Fourth Quarter of Year Two. The process is changing, and these changes make the revision of the limits moot. We do not need to polish these limits. Instead, we need to understand what they reveal about the changes in the process. Computations will not help things here. Action is required.

FOUR QUESTIONS

Many years ago, Perry Regier formulated a set of four questions to use in determining if you need to revise the limits.

1. Do the data display a distinctly different kind of behavior than in the past?
2. Do you know the reason for this change in behavior?
3. Is the new process behavior desirable?
4. Is it intended and expected that the new behavior will continue?

If the answer to all four questions is yes, then it is appropriate to revise the limits based on data collected since the change in the process.

If the answer to question 1 is no, then there should be no need for new limits.

If the answer to question 2 is no, then you should be looking for the Assignable Cause instead of tinkering with the limits.

If the answer to question 3 is no, then why are you not working to remove the detrimental Assignable Cause instead of tinkering with the limits?

If the answer to question 4 is no, then you should again be looking for the Assignable Cause instead of tinkering with the limits.

In retrospect, had we used these four questions with the data and limits of Figure 11.1, we would have had four yes answers, and we would have decided to revise these limits, as was done in Figure 11.2.

Remember, the objective is to take the right action on the process. No credit is given for finding the "right number." The rationality of the baseline used for the computation of the limits is much more important than the number of data points contained within the baseline. Remember, the limits of Figure 11.1 used more data than the subsequent limits, but these limits did not represent either the old system or the new system.

DEGREES OF FREEDOM

The priority for choosing a baseline is not the number of data points within that baseline, but rather the rationality of that baseline given the context for the data. However, it is still sometimes helpful to be able to talk about the "degrees of freedom" in your limits.

For an *XmR* Chart with limits based on the *average* of $(k-1)$ moving ranges, the limits will be said to be based upon approximately $0.62\,(k-1)$ degrees of freedom. For an *XmR* Chart with limits based on the *median* of $(k-1)$ moving ranges, the limits will be said to be based upon approximately $0.32\,(k-1)$ degrees of freedom.

Degrees of freedom is statistical jargon for, "How many data did you use and how efficiently did you use them?" These questions are focused on the uncertainty in the estimation of the three-sigma limits. As the number of degrees of freedom go up, the uncertainty in the estimation goes down. Letting *d.f.* represent the degrees of freedom, this inverse relationship can be expressed as:

$$\textit{Uncertainty in Limits} \approx \frac{1}{\sqrt{2\ d.f.}}$$

If we plot the uncertainties versus the degrees of freedom, we get the graph in Figure 11.4 where we see that the first few degrees of freedom correspond to a dramatic drop in the uncertainty of the limits. We reach the point of diminishing returns somewhere around 10 degrees of freedom. After this point, the uncertainty in the limits will change very slowly as additional data are used. By the time we have 30 degrees of freedom the limits will have solidified to the point that additional data are of little use.

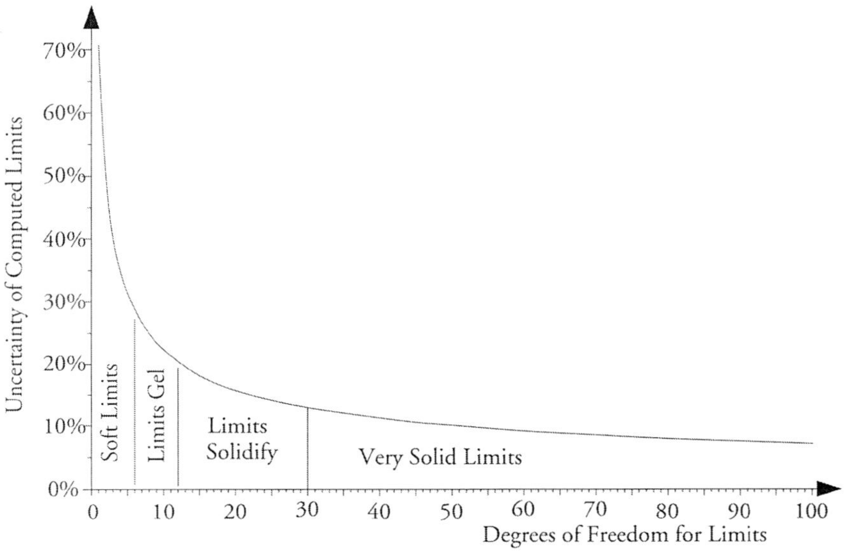

Figure 11.4: Degrees of Freedom and Uncertainty in Computed Limits

Careful consideration of this curve will show why many guidelines suggest using 25 to 30 data points in your baseline period. While such guidelines are not incorrect, they do not address the far more critical question regarding the rationality of the baseline period.

Note also that the curve in Figure 11.4 does not describe the *accuracy* of the limits, but only how the *uncertainty* in the estimated limits drops with increasing degrees of freedom. Limits with many degrees of freedom can be inaccurate because they are based on inflated or biased values. For example, the limits in Figure 11.2, with only two and four degrees of freedom respectively, are more descriptive of the process than the limits in Figure 11.1 which had seven degrees of freedom. While the limits in Figure 11.2 have more uncertainty than those in Figure 11.1, they are more accurate both mathematically and conceptually.

SOFTWARE ISSUES

Some software will automatically recompute the limits using all of the data every time a new data point is added. The implicit assumption behind this recomputation is that the new point should be included in the computation in order to increase the degrees of freedom for the limits. But what if the new point is a signal of a change? As we saw with the limits in Figure 11.1, it is more important to have a rational baseline than it is to use more data. If you can turn off this recomputation option in your software, you should do so. The software does not know whether a given baseline is rational or not. ***Do not let the software choose the points to be included in your baseline.***

Other software will automatically use the last 30 points (or the last 30 subgroups) to recompute the limits every time a new point (or subgroup) is added to the chart. This provides you with an ever shifting frame of reference for your chart. Once more, the most important aspect of your choice of baseline is that it should be rational. Admittedly, we may start off with an arbitrary baseline, as I did in Figure 11.1. But as we learn about the process, we can usually define a baseline that makes sense in the context of the data. Once we have done this, the use of this fixed baseline allows us to interpret the subsequent data intelligently. A sliding baseline that is constantly updated is simply another triumph of computation over common sense. ***If you can turn off the constant recomputation option in your software, you need to do so. Otherwise, get new software.***

Use, and revise, the limits in order to tell the story contained in the data with greater clarity. Whenever the context will allow it, using 20 or 30 data points is desirable, but it is not absolutely necessary.

CHAPTER TWELVE

BUT THE LIMITS ARE TOO WIDE!

When administrative and managerial data are placed on an *XmR* Chart, the first reaction will frequently be that the limits are far too wide—"We have to react before we get to that limit." So what are we to do when this happens? Are the limits really too wide? There are three cases to consider: the data are full of noise; the data are full of signals; and the data, in turn, represent different processes.

THE DATA ARE FULL OF NOISE

Administrative and managerial data tend to be report-card data. The measures are accumulated across departments, across plants, across regions, and even across countries before being presented for consumption by the executives. At each stage, as the data are aggregated, the noise of each data stream is also being aggregated into the total, so that by the time the finished value is presented, it has a lot of noise in the background. For example, consider the quarterly sales values for one company shown in Figure 12.1.

If they ever reached the upper limit on the *X* Chart, they would be the darling of Wall Street. Conversely, if the sales dropped to equal the lower limit they would be in serious trouble. So are these limits too wide? Not really. These wide limits are simply warning the

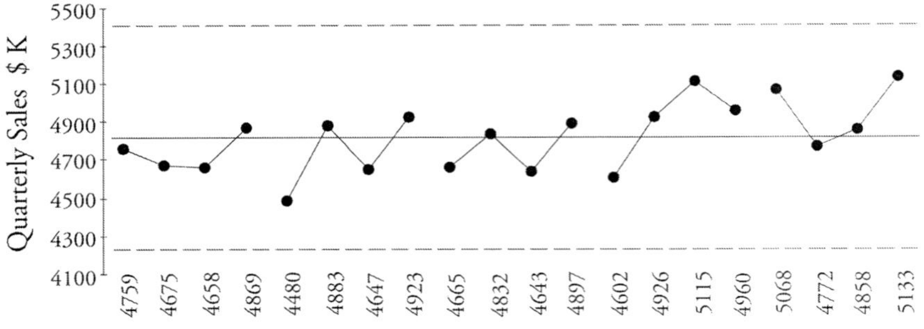

Figure 12.1: *X* Chart: Quarterly Sales for All Regions for Years 01 to 05

reader that it would be a mistake to react to changes in these values.

These data are so full of noise that you will never be able to explain why the sales have gone up or why they have gone down. While you may believe that the advertising campaign helped the sales, or that the recession is hurting sales, these data contain far too much noise to allow you to demonstrate that any particular cause had any specific effect upon the sales! In short, while report-card data result in report-card charts, most of the time report-card data are too full of noise to allow you to identify what needs to be done to change things.

So while report-card charts are valid, they will often have very wide limits because the data are full of noise. The wide limits serve as a warning that it is virtually impossible to assign an explanation to why a point goes up or why it goes down—the routine variation inherent in the data stream itself is sufficient to be the cause of any particular increase or decrease. While movement in one direction may be good and movement in the other direction may be bad, ***most report-card data are too full of noise to be used to run the business!***

Any failure to appreciate this point will result in the interpretation of noise as if it amounted to signals, which is the first type of mistake that can be made in interpreting data.

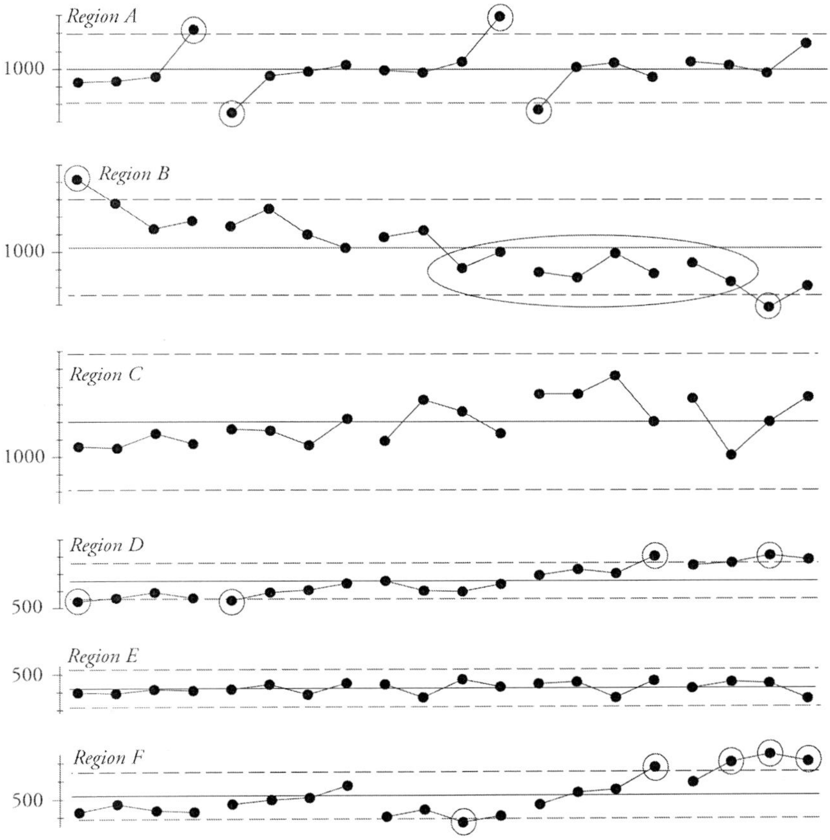

Figure 12.2: *X* Charts: Quarterly Sales by Region for Years 1 to 5

Consider the regional sales that were combined to give the graph in Figure 12.1. These six time-series are shown on their own *X* Charts in Figure 12.2.

There we see many signals of changes that were occurring at the regional level. These signals were all lost in the noise when these six time series were combined into the report-card measure in Figure 12.1. Thus, one way to deal with data that have very wide limits is to disaggregate the time-series into its constituent components and consider each component separately.

THE DATA ARE FULL OF SIGNALS

Because of the way the limits are computed, they can become inflated whenever changes become commonplace.

Moving ranges are used in order to separate the exceptional variation from the routine variation. When we compute limits using either the average or the median of the moving ranges, we hope to dilute the impact of any exceptional variation that is present. *Thus, in the end, the computations implicitly assume that exceptional variation will be an occasional thing.* As more and more of the moving ranges are affected by some Assignable Cause it will become harder to distinguish between exceptional variation and routine variation. Finally, at some point, the exceptional variation may become so commonplace that it will look like routine variation to the computations.

So how can we tell if the data are full of signals? In some cases the context will provide the key. In others, we will need a reference period, where the process is operated without the influence of the Assignable Cause, before we can see that the data are full of signals.

As an example of the first case, where the context will provide a clue that the data are full of signals, we use the data for neonatal autopsies for one hospital over a ten year period. The data are shown in Table 12.1 and the *X* Chart is in Figure 12.3.

The limits of 99.4% and 23.4% provide no discrimination here. They are far too wide for any practical purpose. However, any process that changes from 92% in one year to 36% in another year is clearly not the same from year to year. The limits do not show these changes as signals because these data are full of signals. Fortunately, limits are not needed here since common sense is sufficient. The first

Table 12.1: Neonatal Autopsies

Year	1	2	3	4	5	6	7	8	9	10
Fatalities	38	60	67	57	49	46	53	45	32	40
Autopsies	35	44	46	32	36	24	30	16	13	26
Autopsy %	92%	73%	69%	56%	73%	52%	57%	36%	41%	65%

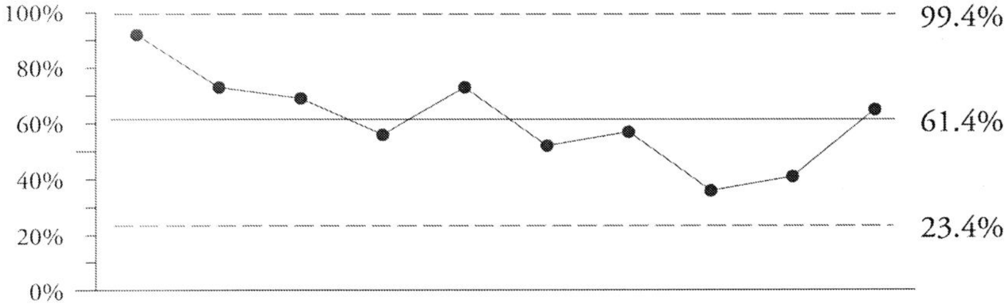

Figure 12.3: *X* Chart for Neonatal Autopsies

principle for understanding data is that no data have any meaning apart from their context. This means that context must always be the starting point for any analysis. Here the context tells us that this process is changing from year to year.

One author suggested placing these data on a *p*-Chart as a way of fixing these wide limits. However, since the likelihood of a neonatal fatality being autopsied is not likely to be the same for all fatalities in a given year, these data do not satisfy the requirements for a *p*-Chart.

So how does this differ from the situation where the data are full of noise? When we are working with a highly aggregated metric, as in Figure 12.1, wide limits are most likely to be due to excessive noise. When we are working with a simple, localized metric, as in Figure 12.3, wide limits may be due to changing conditions from period to period. To discern which is the case will require judgment, experience, and contextual knowledge.

With annual values like those in Table 12.1 it is often helpful to break the data down into shorter time periods. Given the small

Table 12.2: Neonatal Autopsies By Quarter

Year	1				2				3			
Quarter	I	II	III	IV	I	II	III	IV	I	II	III	IV
Fatalities	17	6	8	7	9	17	11	23	17	15	17	18
Autopsy	16	5	8	6	6	12	7	19	9	12	12	13
Percentage	94.1	83.3	100.	85.7	66.7	70.6	63.6	82.6	52.9	80.0	70.6	72.2
Year	4				5				6			
Quarter	I	II	III	IV	I	II	III	IV	I	II	III	IV
Fatalities	13	16	18	10	6	10	13	10	13	3	17	13
Autopsy	7	8	13	4	4	8	10	4	7	2	10	5
Percentage	53.9	50.0	72.2	40.0	75.0	80.0	76.9	40.0	53.8	66.7	58.8	38.5
Year	7				8				9			
Quarter	I	II	III	IV	I	II	III	IV	I	II	III	IV
Fatalities	10	13	13	17	15	8	7	15	8	9	9	6
Autopsy	3	7	8	12	6	1	3	6	3	4	5	1
Percentage	30.0	53.8	61.5	70.6	40.0	12.5	42.9	40.0	37.5	44.4	55.6	16.7
Year	10											
Quarter	I	II	III	IV								
Fatalities	10	10	10	10								
Autopsy	6	7	6	7								
Percentage	60.0	70.0	60.0	70.0								

counts, quarterly summaries would be about as far as we should go (monthly values would involve very small counts indeed). Table 12.2 shows what the quarterly data for Neonatal Autopsies might look like.

If we use the first year as our baseline, the *XmR* Chart will have an average of 0.908 and an average moving range of 0.139. This will give a lower limit for the *X* Chart of 0.538, and an upper limit that exceeds 1.00. With limits of 54% to 100% this chart will hardly provide the most precise analysis, *but it is sufficient to begin to tell the story contained in the data*, as may be seen in Figure 12.4.

With three out of four points closer to the lower limit than the central line, Year Two can be said to be different from Year One. This impression that a change has occurred is confirmed when the first point of Year Three falls below the lower limit.

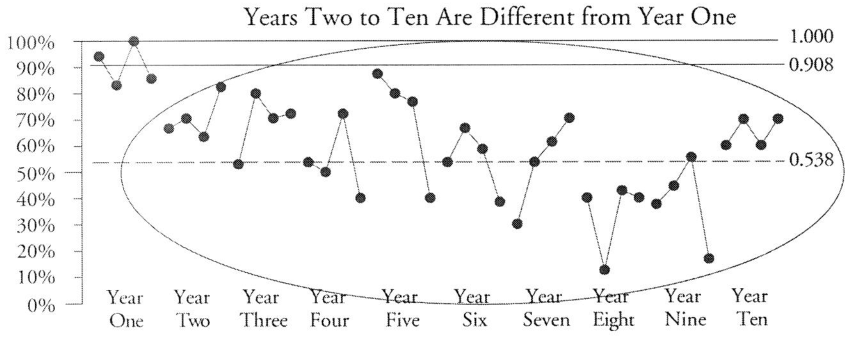

Figure 12.4: *X* Chart for Quarterly Neonatal Autopsies

But wait. The limits in Figure 12.4 are only based on 4 points! Yes, that is true, but this analysis is sufficient to show that a change has occurred. The objective is to gain insight and share it with others, and to this end, the best analysis is the simplest analysis that provides the needed insight.

It is not a matter of using the right amount of data or computing the best estimates of the limits, but rather using the data in context to tell the story of what is happening. The chart in Figure 12.3 failed to do this because it used annual values and the year-to-year changes inflated the limits. The chart in Figure 12.4 succeeds in doing this because, in spite of the small counts involved and the small number of points used in computing the limits, the limits were not inflated by the year-to-year differences.

In fact, the chart in Figure 12.4 can be improved by using multiple sets of limits to tell the story. Since Years Two and Three look different from Year One, use them to compute new limits. Now Years Four, Five, Six, and Seven may be seen to be detectably different from Years Two and Three. So compute new limits using Years Four though Seven. Now Years Eight and Nine are seen to be detectably

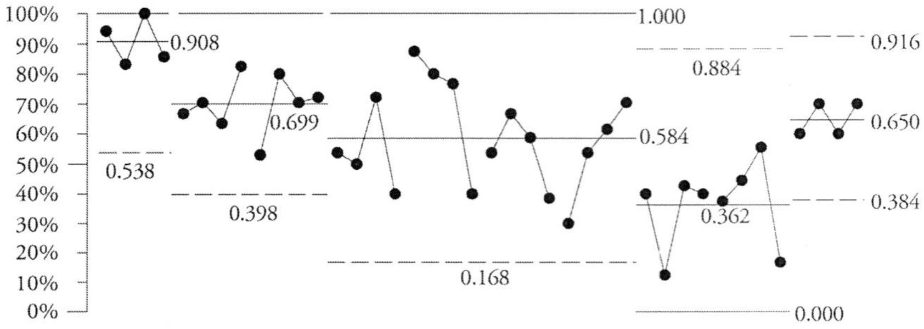

Figure 12.5: Revised *X* Chart for Quarterly Neonatal Autopsies

different from Years Four, Five, Six, and Seven. So compute new limits using Years Eight and Nine. Now we see that Year Ten is detectably different from Years Eight and Nine, and so we compute new limits using Year Ten. In this way we end up with Figure 12.5.

In Year One the autopsy rate was over 90%. In Years Two and Three it dropped to 70%. In Years Four through Seven it dropped to 58%. In Years Eight and Nine it dropped to 36%. In Year Ten it went back up to 65%.

None of the limits obtained here are very tight. This is because these data still contain a substantial amount of noise. However, this does not stop us from telling the story in these data when we disaggregate the annual summaries and use the limits intelligently. Here, the interesting question is what happened at the end of Years One, Three, Seven, and Nine. It turns out that each of these points corresponds to a change in personnel. In this hospital it was the job of the chaplain to obtain permission for a neonatal autopsy, and the different chaplains did this job differently.

The primary question of data analysis is the question of homogeneity. If the data are reasonably homogeneous, then we are justified in assuming that the underlying process is being operated predictably, and in using the central line, limits, and other statistics computed from the data to characterize that underlying process.

However, if the data show evidence that the process is changing, the focus shifts from using the computed values to characterize a single process to one of using the computed values to detect when and how the process is changing. Until we understand the story told by the data, we will not know how to operate the process up to its full potential. Here there is no such thing as computing the right limits or having enough data.

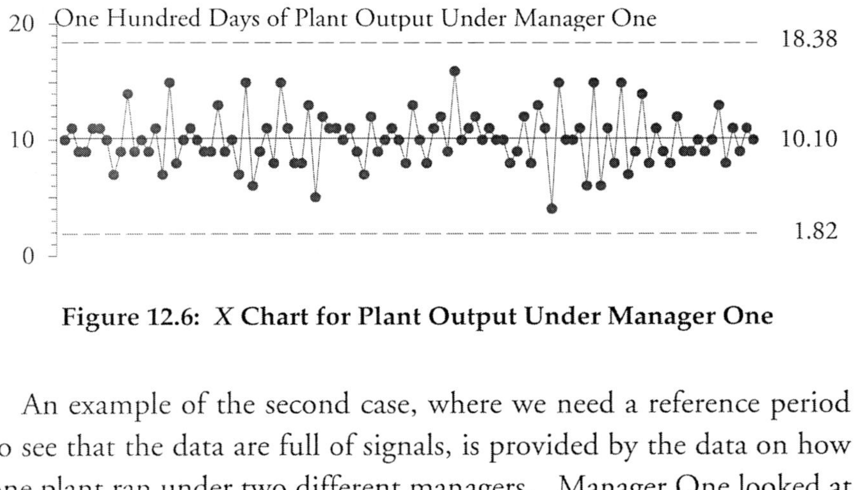

Figure 12.6: *X* Chart for Plant Output Under Manager One

An example of the second case, where we need a reference period to see that the data are full of signals, is provided by the data on how one plant ran under two different managers. Manager One looked at the Productivity Reports each morning to see how the plant performed. If the output for the final, bottleneck step fell short of the scheduled amount, then he would make adjustments in manpower and operations for the current day. On the whole he ended up making adjustments over 80 percent of the time. Figure 12.6 shows the *X* Chart for the plant output for 100 days under Manager One.

Manager Two succeeded Manager One. He also looked at the Productivity Report each morning. However, he plotted the output values on an *X* Chart and only made adjustments to the operation of the plant when a point went outside the limits. Figure 12.7 shows the *X* Chart for the plant output under Manager Two. Manager Two had one-third less variation than Manager One along with a higher average output, using the same work force in the same plant.

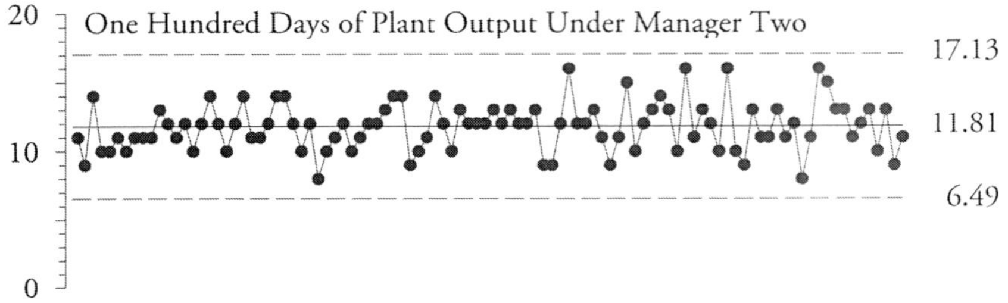

Figure 12.7: *X* Chart for Plant Output Under Manager Two

Manager One's adjustments were so frequent (over 80 percent of the time) that the impact of those changes looked exactly like routine variation to the computations. Manager One had 150% of the variation displayed by Manager Two, along with a lower average daily output, yet his data appear to come from a predictable process.

In order for an XmR Chart to work it is important that successive values be logically comparable. This means, among other things, that the conditions under which the successive values are obtained will need to have remained the same from period to period.

If the time periods have been made so large that the system is bound to have changed from one period to the next, or if the data were collected while the process was deliberately being adjusted or changed, then the resulting data are likely to be full of signals, and the limits may be inflated by those signals.

THE DATA REPRESENT DIFFERENT PROCESSES

Here the data occur in a natural time order, and yet they represent two or more conditions, resulting in an apples-to-oranges time series. When this happens we have a special case of the problem where the data are full of signals.

The example for this case comes from an allergist who had his patients track their lung congestion using a Peak Expiratory Flow Rate (PEFR) Gauge. The patient would exhale as hard as possible through the gauge, and the gauge would record the flow rate in liters per minute. The protocol consisted of the patient getting one flow rate in the morning and one flow rate in the evening. The morning reading was to be obtained prior to taking any medication. The evening reading was to be taken 15 minutes after using the bronchodilator inhaler. The sequence of values would thus represent two states: A.M. pre-med and P.M. post-med. Looking at these data as a time series, the physician tried to place these values on an *XmR* Chart. The resulting *X* Chart is shown in Figure 12.8.

The wide limits are a result of the large daily swings. This chart violates the guideline given at the end of the previous section. No progress was made in using the charts in clinical practice until the physician started charting the A.M. pre-med values alone.

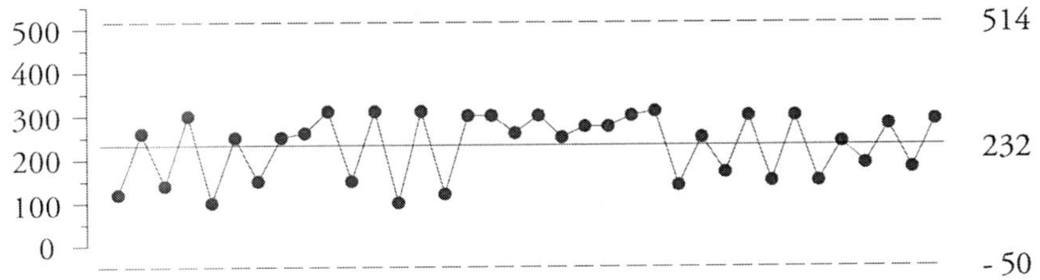

Figure 12.8: *X* Chart for A.M. & P.M. PEFR Scores for One Patient

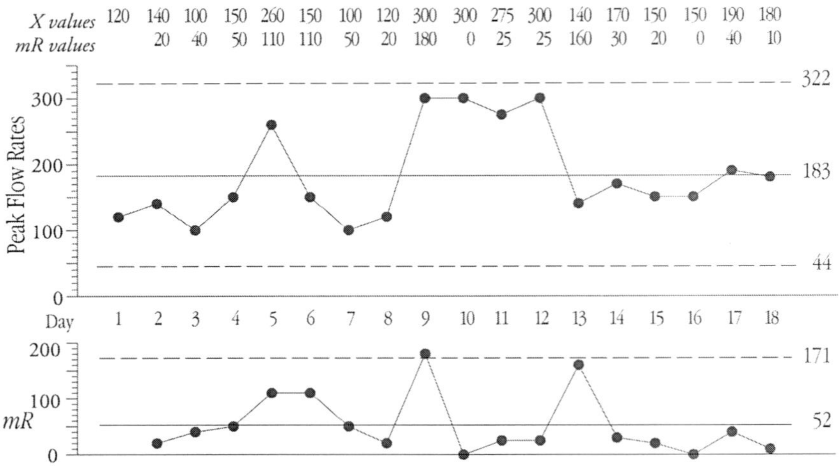

Figure 12.9: *XmR* Chart for A.M. PEFR Scores for One Patient

The *XmR* Chart for the A.M. pre-med PEFR scores for this patient is shown in Figure 12.9. There we see an upper limit that is consistent with her predicted best score and a lower limit that is consistent with her medical history. The four good days corresponded to a weekend visit by the patient to her aunt's house, where her symptoms essentially disappeared. This realization provided the stimulus to start changing this girl's home environment, which, in turn, proved to be the beginning of a turnaround in her struggle with asthma.

When the data are organized in a rational manner, the chart can begin to tell the story contained within the data. But when the data are thrown onto the chart without regard for the context of the data, the resulting chart can be useless.

SUMMARY

Thus, it is possible for the limits on an *XmR* Chart to be inflated to the point that the limits are essentially useless. Since there are two different causes, it is critical that you understand both how this happens and what you can do about it.

If the data are full of signals, then the wide limits are incorrect and the organization of the chart is at fault. *Here it is up to the user to organize the data in such a way that the charts can be useful.* In order for the *XmR* Chart to work we need to make sure that successive values are logically comparable. Occasionally it might be helpful to use the Median Moving Range as explained in the next chapter, but the rational organization of the data is fundamental to having useful charts.

If the data are full of noise, then the measure will be of little use in running the business. It may be an important report-card measure, but it still cannot be used to identify what caused the values to change. *Here it is not the chart that is at fault, but rather the idea that you can make use of the data in spite of the noise they contain.* The failure to understand this point will inevitably result in Manager One Syndrome.

Manager Two did one thing differently than Manager One—he did not react to the noise in the data. By avoiding Mistake One he did not create any man-made chaos. He got the system to operate up to its full potential by simply avoiding the unnecessary adjustments that consumed so much of Manager One's time and energy.

It is interesting to note that "Manager One Syndrome" is encouraged by the emphasis on looking at all of the current values together on a monthly "dashboard." This current fad does encourage the use of multiple measures rather than reacting to each value separately, but it still lacks the filter that separates the signals (where there is something to be learned) from the noise (where there is no change from previous months). With the monthly dashboard any two numbers that are not the same are thought to be different. Unfortunately, this is not true.

All data contain noise.

Some data also contain signals.

Until you can differentiate between the noise of routine variation and the signals of exceptional variation you are likely to be misled by the noise.

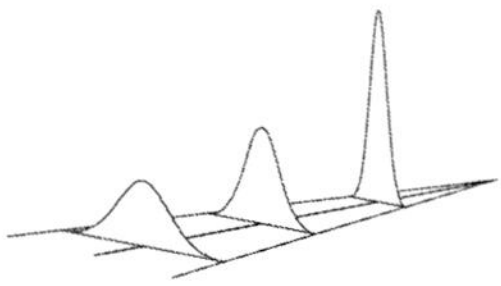

CHAPTER THIRTEEN

WHEN DO WE USE A MEDIAN MOVING RANGE?

While the Average Moving Range will usually be sufficient to obtain reasonable limits for an *XmR* Chart, there are times when we like to shift over to using the Median Moving Range instead. The purpose of this chapter is to explain when this is appropriate.

We prefer to use the Average Moving Range as the default computation because it is 100 percent efficient. When we arrange the data into pseudo-subgroups of size two, and use the *average* of the two-point moving ranges to estimate dispersion, we will have extracted *all* of the within-subgroup information about dispersion that is contained in the data.

However, if a substantial proportion of the moving ranges have been inflated by changes in the process, then the efficiency of the average will end up inflating the Average Moving Range and result in inflated limits for the *XmR* Chart. Since inflated limits simply make the chart more conservative, this is not always a problem. Any signals found using inflated limits are almost surely real. But inflated limits can result in our missing some signals.

This is where the lower efficiency of the median is useful. Medians are less severely affected by extreme values than are averages, and in

Table 13.1: The Hot Metal Transit Times in Minutes

40	45	125	100	40	40	100	65	55	40	125	65	40	45	95
105	45	110	40	50	120	45	65	105	35	70	55	25	50	55
50	40	40	45	55	50	45	125	55	100	40	70	40	40	110
55	50	30	50	105	45	45	55	50	25	65	60	60	55	70
55	45	100	60	45	145	45	50	65	180	60	45	35	35	55
55	55	50	120	35	45	35	45	55	50	70	45	75	60	45
60	40	60	40	50	60	65	95	65	60	50	25	25	100	50
60	45	35	40	30	180	50	30	30	30	65	130	80	20	45
65	65	45	40	50	25	120	30	115	50	85	40	35	40	40
55	50	25	75	55	50									

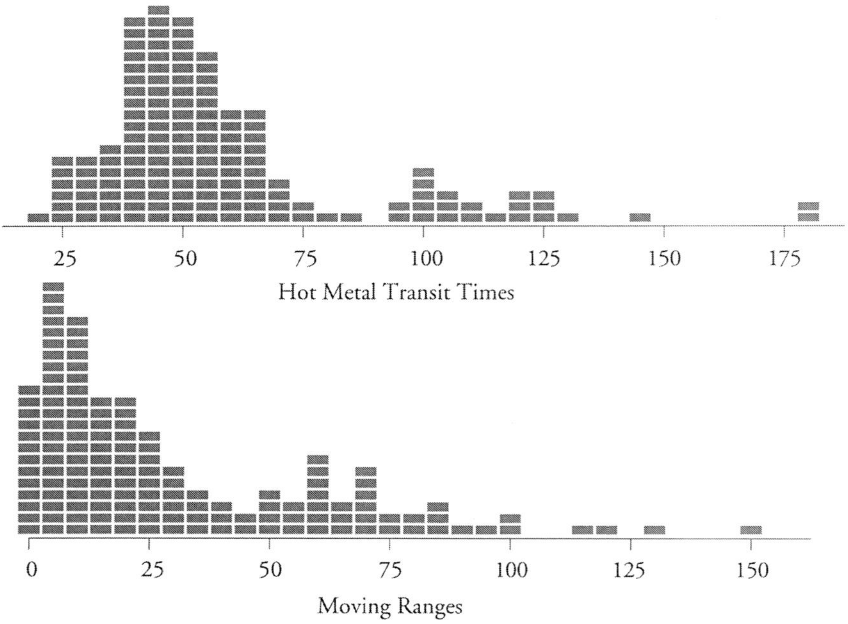

Figure 13.1: Histograms for Transit Times and Their Moving Ranges

the presence of extreme values, a median will provide a better measure of location than an average. So, if you have reason to think that the Average Moving Range may have been inflated by an excessive number of large moving ranges, or even a few very large moving ranges, you may switch over to using the Median Moving Range.

To illustrate the impact of this we will use the Hot Metal Transit Times from Chapter Eight. The data are shown in rows in Table 13.1. The histograms for both the transit times and the moving ranges are shown in Figure 13.1.

Both histograms have at least two humps or mounds, which suggests that at least two different processes are being mixed together here. For the transit times the average is 59.9 minutes while the median is 50 minutes. Which provides the better measure of the location of the main mound? For the moving ranges the average is 31 minutes and the median is 20 minutes. Which of these values provides the better measure of location for the main mound of the moving ranges?

Using the Average and the Average Moving Range we get an upper limit for the *X* Chart of 142.4 minutes and an upper range limit of 101.3 minutes. In Figure 13.2 only 3 of the 141 transit times exceed these limits. While these are almost certainly real signals, the question remains: Have we missed some signals by using these limits?

A histogram with two mounds is one of the indicators that we might want to use the Median Moving Range. In this case we might

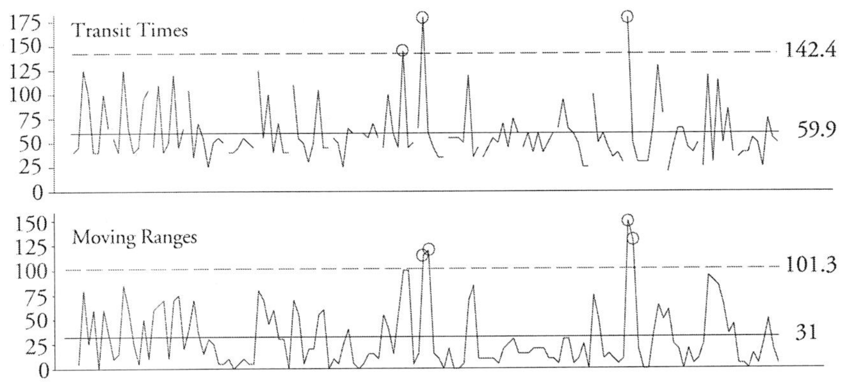

Figure 13.2: *XmR* Chart Based on Average and Average Moving Range

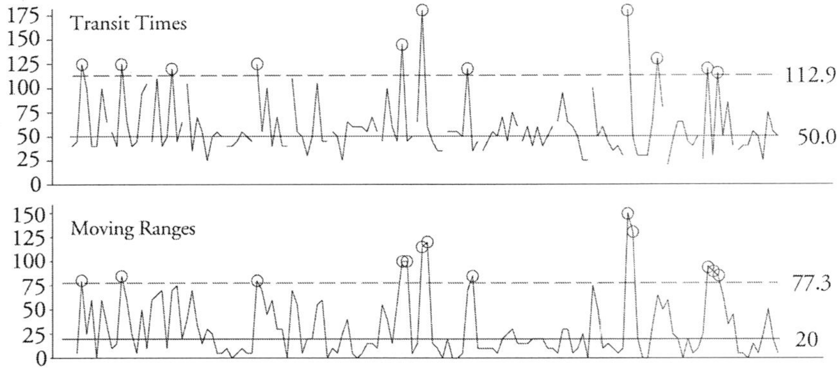

Figure 13.3: *XmR* Chart Based on Median and Median Moving Range

also want to use the Median as the central line for the *X* Chart.

Using the Median and the Median Moving Range we get an upper limit for the *X* Chart of 112.9 minutes and an upper range limit of 77.3 minutes. Figure 13.3 shows that 11 transit times and 13 moving ranges exceed these limits. Here the Median and Median Moving Range provide better summary values, which result in limits that are more sensitive.

The Hot Metal Transit Time Data are also seen in Chapters Eight and Sixteen, where the limits based upon the Median and the Median Moving Range are used. Another example of the use of the Median Moving Range is provided by the *X* Chart in Figure 18.3.

So we tend to use the Average Moving Range as our primary means of computing the limits for an *X* Chart, and we shift to using the Median Moving Range only when we suspect that the presence of several excessively large moving ranges may have inflated the Average Moving Range. This shift is a matter of judgment on the part of the user.

CHAPTER FOURTEEN

WHAT CAN BE CONSIDERED A SIGNAL?

A signal of a change in the underlying process can show up on a process behavior chart in several different ways. Some of these signals are fairly straightforward, while others will only become apparent when the structure of the data is taken into account. For this reason, it is very important that the person using the chart takes the time to interpret the chart in the context of the data. While points outside the three-sigma limits are obvious signals of change, any persistent or coherent pattern that makes sense in the context of the data may also be interpreted as a signal of a change.

It is this *context based interpretation* that makes the process behavior chart so powerful. By displaying the data in a comprehensible format, so that the context can be aligned with the data, the charts minimize the effort and time required to understand the data. This is why it always risky to let the software interpret the chart. The software does not and cannot know the context. For this reason, I always turn off all detection rules in any software program I am using, and I strongly recommend that you do the same.

When looking for patterns that make sense in the context of the data, it is useful to have some threshold to use so that you will not accidentally misinterpret noise as a signal. The pattern detection guideline provides such a threshold.

> **The Pattern Detection Guideline:** Any pattern consisting of two, three, or more points, which is repeated eight times in succession, is highly unlikely to be due to routine variation.

Any such recurring patterns are telling you about systematic variation in your data, and they should be interpreted in the context of those data.

An example of a repeating pattern signal is shown in Figure 14.1. Each of three operators would produce five batches of rubber compound per shift. A sample of each batch was tested in the lab, and the five values for each operator were used to create a subgroup of size five for an Average and Range Chart. The resulting Range Chart is shown. Each range value in Figure 14.1 shows the variation in the batches produced by each operator on each shift.

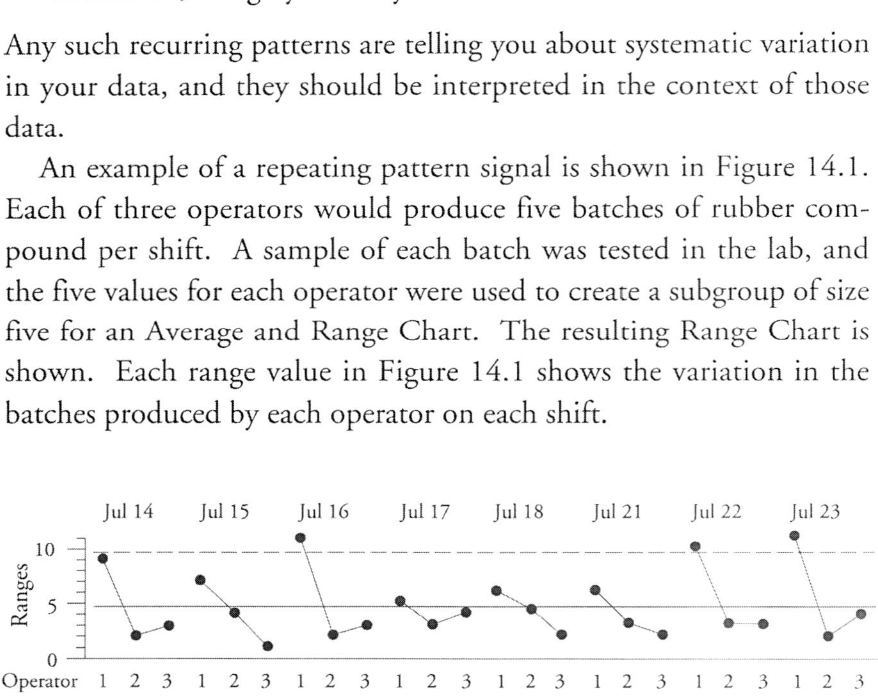

Figure 14.1: Range Chart for Times to Maximum Torque

The three point pattern of high-low-low that repeats itself eight times makes it clear beyond a shadow of a doubt that the first operator has much more variation in his batches than do the other two.

While Operator One had 30 years of experience in running a rubber mill, and while his supervisor considered him to be a model worker, his batches simply were not consistent in quality. Upon investigation the supervisor discovered that Operator One had lost his visual acuity to the point that he was effectively blind! He could not see well enough to mix the rubber and so, mindful of the hazard implicit in operating a rubber mill, he simply started each batch and stepped back. The excessive variation came from the fact that he was not really mixing each batch. Until someone took the time to discover the pattern and ask the right question, no one, except Operator One, knew that they had a blind man running a piece of equipment that could maim or kill its operator.

While there are three points above the upper range limit, none of the algebraic detection rules given below would have found the *pattern* seen in Figure 14.1. This is why it is essential to always interpret the charts in the context of the data.

Having said this, we now turn to the detection rules you will encounter in your software. The most widely used set of detection rules is a set that was published in the Western Electric Handbook in 1956. This set of four detection rules starts with a point outside the three-sigma limits and then adds three run-test rules.

THE WESTERN ELECTRIC ZONE TESTS

> **Detection Rule One:** Look for a dominant Assignable Cause whenever a single point falls outside the three-sigma limits on either the *X* Chart or the *mR* Chart.

The first and most obvious signal of a process change would be one or more *points outside the three-sigma limits.* Since three-sigma limits will filter out virtually all of the routine variation, any point outside the three-sigma limits is a potential signal. Moreover, the further a point is outside the limits, the stronger the evidence that a change has occurred. False alarms, when they occur, will be rare and will tend to be just barely outside the limits, so as the number of

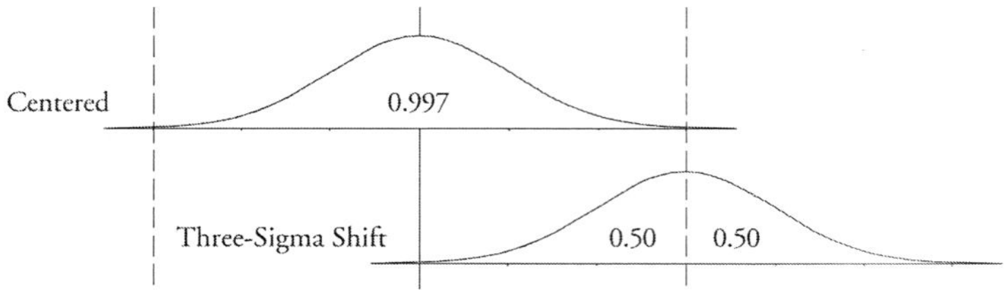

Figure 14.2: Detection Rule One Will Find Large Shifts

points outside the limits increases, and as their distance outside the limits increases, your confidence will increase that the process is, indeed, being operated in an unpredictable manner.

As may be seen in Figure 14.2, when the process average has shifted by three-sigma units or more, the chance of a point falling outside the three-sigma limits on the *X* Chart will exceed 50 percent. This why Detection Rule One is especially effective with large shifts.

Since Detection Rule One is good for large shifts, the following detection rules were added in order to increase the sensitivity of the process behavior chart to smaller shifts. Since smaller shifts are inherently harder to detect, and therefore require more evidence, the following detection rules are run-tests. That is, they use a sequence of values that satisfy some criteria to detect smaller shifts in the underlying process.

> **Detection Rule Two:** Whenever two out of three successive values on the *X* Chart are both on the same side of the central line and are both more than two sigma units away from the central line, you should look for the cause of a moderate shift in the underlying process.

Detection Rule Two is commonly referred to as a *run beyond two sigma.* It can only be used when the notion of sequence makes sense for your chart. It cannot be used with the *mR* Chart.

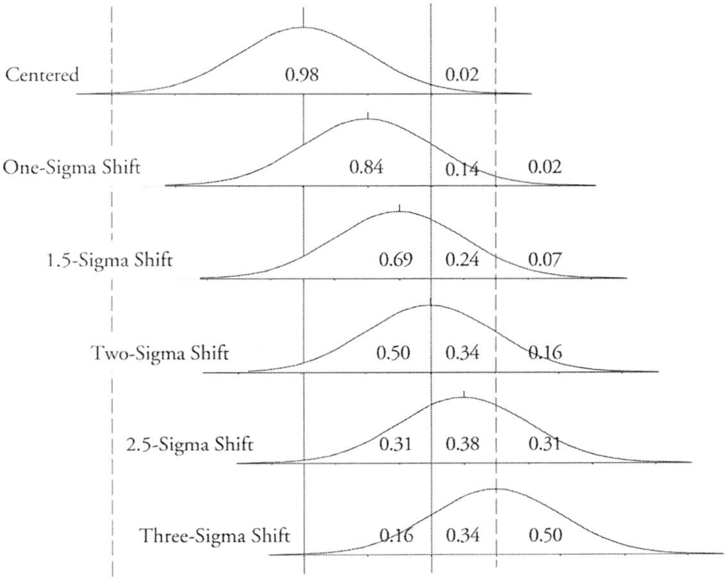

Figure 14.3: Rule Two Will Be Most Sensitive to Two-Sigma Shifts

Inspection of Figure 14.3 will show that Rule Two will tend to be most sensitive to shifts in the neighborhood of two sigma. Shifts of this size will tend to maximize the chances of a point falling beyond the two-sigma line while the chance of going beyond the three-sigma limit is still fairly small. Larger shifts will tend to be detected by Rule One. Smaller shifts are less likely to satisfy Detection Rule Two.

In interpreting Detection Rule Two, the third point can fall anywhere. Only the two values have to satisfy the two conditions.

> **Detection Rule Three:** Whenever four out of five successive values on the *X* Chart are on the same side of the central line and are also more than one sigma unit away from the central line, you should look for the cause of a small to moderate shift in the underlying process.

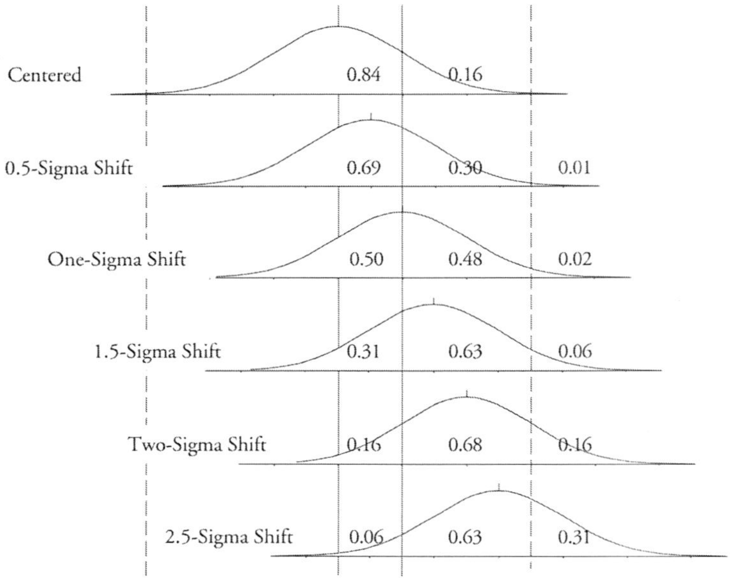

Figure 14.4: Rule Three Will Be Most Sensitive to 1.5-Sigma Shifts

Detection Rule Three is commonly referred to as a *run beyond one sigma*. This rule can only be used when the notion of sequence makes sense, and it cannot be used with the *mR* Chart.

In interpreting Detection Rule Three, the fifth point can fall anywhere. Only the four values have to satisfy the two conditions.

As may be seen in Figure 14.4, Detection Rule Three will be most sensitive to shifts in the neighborhood of 1.0 to 1.5 sigma. Larger shifts will tend to be detected by Rules One or Two. Smaller shifts become increasingly hard to detect.

> **Detection Rule Four:** Whenever eight successive values on the *X* Chart all fall on the same side of the central line, you should look for the cause of a small but sustained shift in the underlying process.

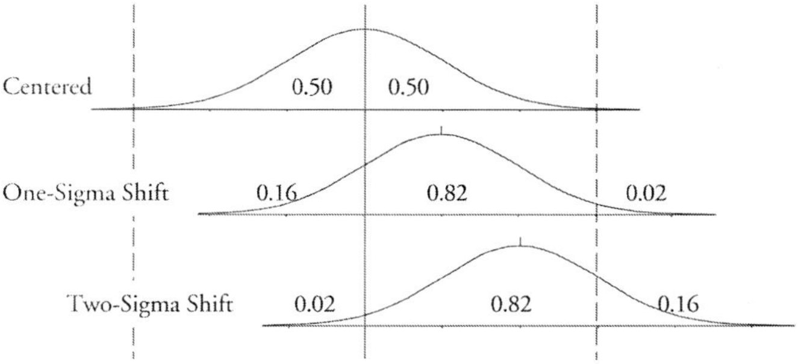

Figure 14.5: Rule Four Will Be Most Sensitive to One-Sigma Shifts

Detection Rule Four is commonly referred to as a *run about the central line.* This detection rule is most sensitive to shifts in the neighborhood of 1.0 sigma. With small shifts we have a small chance of a point going outside the limits, but a large chance that they will all be on the same side of the central line. As the shifts get larger, Detection Rules One, Two, and Three, with their ability to detect signals with fewer data, will tend to dominate Detection Rule Four.

Thus, these rules look for different things. While Rule One looks for large process changes, Rules Two, Three, and Four look for successively smaller sustained changes.

Another difference between these rules lies in the way they work. While Rule One depends upon only upon a single value, Rules Two, Three, and Four depend upon sequences of values. This means that we cannot use Rules Two, Three and Four unless our sequence of values makes sense. When we plot our data in time order, the notion of sequence does make sense, and this is not a problem. However, if we plot our data in some arbitrary order, then the notion of sequence vanishes, and we cannot use the three run-test rules.

While Rule One may be used with either the *X* Chart or the *mR* Chart, Rules Two, Three, and Four may only be used with the *X*

Chart. This is because of the nature of the moving ranges—the computation of the successive differences creates a correlation structure which will tend to create an excess number of false alarms when run-tests are applied to the *mR* Chart. Since we do not want to be misled by false alarms, we simply cannot use any run-test with the *mR* Chart.

With subgrouped data, you may use all four detection rules with an Average Chart. You may also use all four detection rules on the high side of a Range Chart. Because of the skewed histogram typical of subgroup ranges, run-tests applied to the low side of a Range Chart are not as reliable as they are in the other cases.

While Rules One and Four may be used without additional computations, Rules Two and Three require the computation of the one-sigma and two-sigma lines for the *X* Chart. This is not a problem for software, but it is an added burden when doing charts by hand. For this reason the most commonly used detection rules are Rules One and Four. The complementary nature of these two rules allows them to work well together. In fact, you will seldom need more than these two rules.

I will generally use Rules One and Four, and if I happen to see something that might qualify as a signal under Rules Two or Three, I will then bring these two rules out and apply them to my data. If the data will qualify with any of these rules, you are justified in taking the time to look for an Assignable Cause of exceptional variation.

OTHER DETECTION RULES

Most of the software today will have additional detection rules such as rules for runs up and runs down, sawtooths, mixtures, and various patterns. Using a battery of such run tests is like refusing to give up. Use enough detection rules, and even a table of random numbers will show you a signal. Since we want to strike a balance between false alarms (Mistake One) and missed signals (Mistake Two), it is important to limit your use of detection rules.

The Western Electric Zone Tests given here form a coherent set of detection rules which have been proven to provide the maximum boost in sensitivity without an undue increase in the risk of a false alarm. Whenever you want to increase the sensitivity of a process behavior chart, you need only use another rule from the Western Electric Zone Tests. When you are using them all, you will have maximized the sensitivity of your chart.

The fact that there is a limit to the statistical power of any technique means that when you continue to add detection rules beyond the Western Electric Zone Tests you can only increase the false alarm rate. This result has been documented in various journal articles and in practice.

Therefore, you should, in general, avoid the use of additional detection rules. Moreover, with the use of the pattern detection guideline, you should not need to use the whole battery of detection rules. Remember, you are the best pattern recognition device that we know about. And the rationale behind the process behavior chart is to make the data visible so as to engage your brain's ability to spot patterns in the data. While the detection rules may help, it is the picture that is the key element of the process behavior chart.

RECOMMENDATIONS

Use Detection Rules One and Four *manually*. No computations are required, and both are easy to use while looking at the chart.

Use the Pattern Detection Guideline to confirm any suspected patterns within the data.

Turn off all the detection rules in your software. This will remove much of the visual clutter that many software programs have added to the charts, making it easier to actually interpret the chart in context. (You really do not need to always have the one-sigma and two-sigma lines on the chart.) Let the software create the charts, ***but do not let the software interpret the charts.***

Use common sense and context to avoid overanalyzing your charts. Remember, if you torture the data long enough, they will surrender.

Process behavior charts are the interface between you and your data. They become effective only to the extent that they engage your brain and allow you to tell the story contained within your data. To this end, less "chartjunk" frequently results in more understanding.

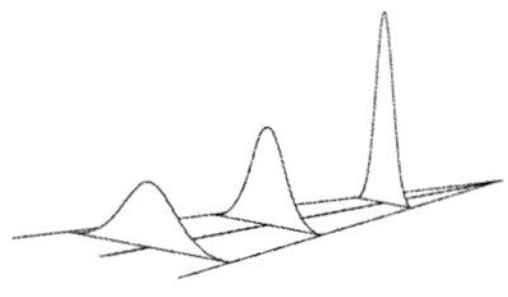

CHAPTER FIFTEEN

WHY A PROCESS BEHAVIOR CHART IS THE FIRST STEP IN DATA ANALYSIS

To explain why a process behavior chart should always be the first step in the analysis of data from any Observational Study we need to first define the four basic questions of statistics. These are the Description, Probability, Inference, and Homogeneity Questions.

THE DESCRIPTION QUESTION

Given a collection of numbers, are there arithmetic values that will summarize the information contained in those numbers in some meaningful way?

The objective is to capture those aspects of the data that are of interest. Intuitive summaries such as totals, averages, and proportions need little explanation. Other summaries that are less commonly used may require some explanation, and even some justification, before they make sense. However, in the end, in order to be effective a descriptive statistic has to make sense—it has to distill some essential characteristic of the data into a value that is both appropriate and understandable. In every case, this distillation takes on the form of some arithmetic operation:

Data + Arithmetic = Statistic

Figure 15.1: The Problem Addressed by the Description Question

As soon as we have said this, it becomes apparent that the justification for computing any given statistic must come from the nature of the data themselves—it cannot come from the arithmetic, nor can it come from the statistic. If the data are a meaningless collection of values, then the summary statistics will also be meaningless—no arithmetic operation can magically create meaning out of nonsense. Therefore, the meaning of any statistic has to come from the context for the data, while the appropriateness of any statistic will depend upon the use we intend to make of that statistic.

This means that before we compute the simplest average, range, or proportion, *it has to make sense to do so.* Thus we have to know the *context* for any collection of values before we can select appropriate summary statistics.

THE PROBABILITY QUESTION

Given a known universe,
what can we say about samples drawn from this universe?

Here we enter the world of deductive logic, the enumeration of possible outcomes, and mathematical models. For simplicity we usually begin with a universe that consists of a bowl filled with known numbers of black and white beads. We then consider the likelihoods of various sample outcomes that might be drawn from this bowl. This is illustrated in Figure 15.2.

Beginning with a Known Universe:

Bowl contains
1000 Black Beads
4000 White Beads

Universe
Proportion Black = 20%

Describe Chance of Sample Outcomes:

The chance of 1 Black in 1 Draw = 0.2

The chance of 2 Blacks in 2 Draws = 0.04

and so on to more complex questions:

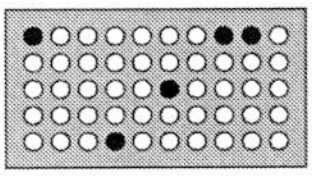

The probability
of getting exactly
Five Black Beads in
a Random Sample
of 50 Beads
is 0.030 or 3%

?

Figure 15.2: The Problem Addressed by the Probability Question

When we reason from a general situation, which is known, to descriptions of specific outcomes, which are presently unknown, we have an argument that is said to be deductive in nature. Deductive logic proceeds from generalities to specifics and always has a correct answer. It is a process of reasoning in which a conclusion follows necessarily from the premises presented.

When we begin with simple universes, such as beads in a bowl, we can often list all of the possible outcomes. From these enumerations it is then possible to characterize the likelihoods of different events.

Since the enumeration of outcomes quickly becomes tedious, shortcuts are sought. By developing mathematical models we can skip the enumeration step and jump directly from the known universe to the likelihoods of different possible outcomes.

As the mathematical models became increasingly sophisticated, and as the methods of computing and approximating the probabilities progressed, the models could be used to characterize more complex problems—problems that could never be handled by the enumeration approach.

Thus, in probability theory we are, in effect, playing a game. We play this game to learn how things behave so that we can use this knowledge later. In introductory classes we restrict ourselves to playing this game with homogeneous and fixed universes.

Obviously, before students can make much headway in probability theory, they will need to be comfortable with deductive logic and mathematical models—two more elements of the foreign language of statistics. While probability theory is a necessary step in the *development* of modern statistical techniques, it is not a step that has to be mastered in order to analyze data effectively.

THE INFERENCE QUESTION

Given an unknown universe, and given a sample
that is known to have been drawn from that unknown universe,
and given that we know everything about the sample,
what can we say about the unknown universe?

This is usually thought of as the inverse of the problem addressed by the probability question. Here, it is the sample that is known and the universe that is unknown. Now the argument proceeds from the specific to the general, which makes it inductive in nature. Unfortunately, all inductive inference is fraught with uncertainty.

A sample result of 5 black beads and 45 white beads corresponds to

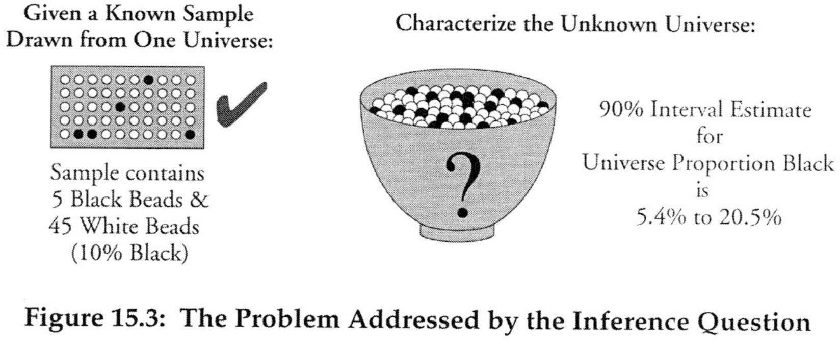

Figure 15.3: The Problem Addressed by the Inference Question

a 90% Interval Estimate of 5.4% to 20.5% for the proportion of black beads in the bowl. The middle ninety percent of the plausible proportions fall in this interval. Thus, with inductive logic there is not a single right answer, but many plausible answers. Any percentage from 5.4% to 20.5% is plausible, given this sample result.

Statistical inference is the realm of tests of hypotheses, confidence intervals, and regression. These techniques allow us to estimate and evaluate the parameters of the unknown universe—proportions, means, and standard deviations. Of course such estimates make sense only when our outcomes are all obtained from a single universe. This assumption of a single universe is equivalent to the assumption that the behavior of these outcomes is described by one probability model. Once we have made this assumption, it is possible to use the probability model in reverse—given this outcome, these are the parameter values that are most consistent with the outcome.

While the mathematics of using the probability model in reverse makes everything seem to be rigorous and scientific, you should note that the whole argument begins with an assumption and ends with an indefinite statement. The *assumption* is that all of the outcomes came from the same universe, and the *indefinite statement* is couched in terms of interval estimates. Again, with inductive inference there is not one right answer, but many plausible answers.

THE HOMOGENEITY QUESTION

Given a collection of observations,
is it reasonable to assume that they came from one universe,
or do they show evidence of having come from multiple universes?

To understand the fundamental nature of the homogeneity question, consider what happens if the collection of values does not come from one universe.

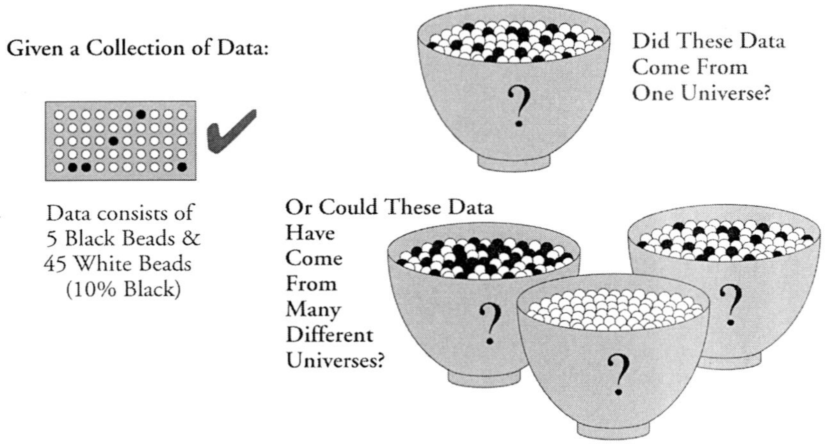

Figure 15.4: The Problem Addressed by the Homogeneity Question

Descriptive statistics are built on the assumption that we can use a single value to characterize a single property for a single universe. If the data come from different sources, how can any single value be used to describe what is, in effect, not one property but many? In Figure 15.4 the sample has 10 percent black. But if the 50 beads are the result of three separate draws from the three bowls at the bottom of Figure 15.4, which bowl is characterized by the sample result? (Notice that the three bowls on the bottom have different numbers of black beads.)

Probability theory is focused on what happens to samples drawn from a known universe. If the data happen to come from different sources, then there are multiple universes with different probability models. If you cannot answer the homogeneity question, then you will not know if you have one probability model or many.

Statistical inference assumes that you have a sample that is known to have come from one universe. If the data come from different sources, what does your interval estimate represent? Which of the multiple universes does it characterize?

Therefore, before you can use the structure and techniques developed to answer the first three problems, you will need to examine your data for evidence of that homogeneity which is implicitly assumed by the use of descriptive statistics, the concepts of probability theory, and the techniques of statistical inference. *This implicit assumption of homogeneity, that is part of everything we do in traditional statistics classes, becomes a real obstacle whenever we try to analyze data.*

HOW TO ANALYZE DATA

When we find evidence of a changing universe in a situation where there should be only one universe we will be unable to learn anything from descriptive statistics. When the universe is changing we cannot gain from statistical inference, nor can we make predictions using probability theory. Any nonhomogeneity in our collection of values completely undermines the techniques developed to answer each of the first three questions. The lack of homogeneity is a signal that unknown things are happening, and until we discover what is happening and remove its causes, we will continue to suffer the consequences. Computations cannot remedy the problem of a lack of homogeneity; action is required.

How can we answer the homogeneity question? We can either *assume* that our data possess the appropriate homogeneity, or we can *examine* them for signs of nonhomogeneity. Since anomalous things happen in even the most carefully controlled experiments, prudence demands that we choose the second course. And the primary tool for examining a collection of values for homogeneity is the process behavior chart.

To examine our data for signs of nonhomogeneity we begin with the tentative assumption that the data are homogeneous and then look for evidence that is inconsistent with this assumption. When we reject the assumption of homogeneity we will have strong evidence which will justify taking action to remedy the situation. When we

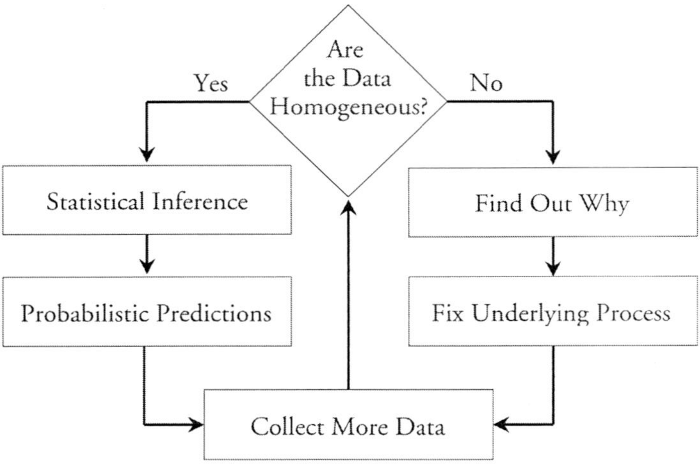

Figure 15.5: Homogeneity Is the Primary Question of Analysis

fail to reject the assumption of homogeneity we will know that any nonhomogeneity present is below the level of detection. While this is a weak result, we will at least have a reasonable basis for proceeding with estimation and prediction.

Thus, for practitioners the first question must always be the question of homogeneity. Given a collection of data, did these data come from one universe? In fact, is it reasonable to assume that there is a universe? Only after this fundamental question has been addressed does the practitioner know how to proceed. If the assumption of a universe is reasonable, then the techniques of statistical inference may be used to characterize that universe, and then, with reasonable estimates of the parameters, probability models may be used to make predictions. But if the assumption of a universe is not justified, the practitioner needs to find out why.

This is not the way classes in statistics are taught, but it is the way you have to do data analysis. Look at your data on some type of process behavior chart. If there are surprises in your data, and there often will be, then learn from these surprises. If there are no surprises, then you may proceed to analyze your data as if they came from a single universe.

CHAPTER SIXTEEN

WHEN DO WE USE SUBGROUPED DATA?

There are two major types of process behavior charts. These are the Chart for Individual Values and Moving Ranges (the *XmR* Chart) and the Average and Range Chart (the *X*-Bar and *R* Chart).

***XmR* Charts tend to be the preferred format whenever the data are obtained one value per time period.** Such data can be said to be "periodically obtained data." This would include managerial, administrative, and service sector data, which tend to occur one value per month; and also process industry data and inspection data, which tend to be one value per batch (or lot), or one number per shift. When the data already have a frequency attached it is logical to use subgroups of size one. Here the *XmR* Chart will let you plot a point every time you get a value. This results in immediate feedback, nothing is hidden, and every point has to sink or swim on its own.

Average and Range Charts tend to be the preferred format when you have the luxury of selecting both the subgroup size and the subgroup frequency. Here it may be helpful to think about a production line making lots of individual items. A sample of these items can be selected with any frequency that makes sense: once a day, once a shift, once an hour, or whatever seems appropriate. At the same time, the number of pieces obtained for each sample could be any reasonable number: two, five, ten, or whatever makes sense. Whenever we have to choose both the sample size and the sample frequency, we tend to use an Average and Range Chart for the data.

RATIONAL SUBGROUPING

Once we have made this choice there is still the question of how to organize these data into k subgroups of size n. The answer to this question is known as rational subgrouping. ***A subgrouping is said to be rational when the data are arranged so that the subgroups are logically homogeneous.*** This means that whenever you place two values together in the same subgroup, you are making a *judgment* that those two values were collected under essentially the same conditions. At the same time, data that might have been collected under different conditions should be placed in different subgroups.

The most common format for rational subgrouping is to use the time-order sequence and to make a subgroup consist of those data that were collected more or less at the same time. In this way, each subgroup should capture the routine, short-term variation, while any process changes will tend to show up between the subgroups.

Notice that rational subgrouping involves judgment. In order to be rational, a subgrouping must take into account the structure of the data, the nature of the process, and the questions of interest to the observer. Rational subgroups do not just happen. They are the result of careful thought. Moreover, they can change over time as the questions of interest change. Rational subgrouping requires practice. Many people have had problems using process behavior charts simply because they were not taught the art of rational subgrouping.

Another aspect of rational subgrouping is a recognition that the two parts of an Average and Range Chart ask different questions of the data. Average Charts look for differences between the subgroups

Table 16.1: Hot Metal Transit Times

Subgroup	Times							Average	Range
1	40	45	125	100	40	40	100	70.00	85
2	65	55	40	125	65	40	45	62.14	85
3	95	105	45	110	40	50	120	80.71	80
4	45	65	105	35	70	55	25	57.14	80
5	50	55	50	40	40	45	55	47.86	15
6	50	45	125	55	100	40	70	69.29	85
7	40	40	110	55	50	30	50	53.57	80
8	105	45	45	55	50	25	65	55.71	80
9	60	60	55	70	55	45	100	63.57	55
10	60	45	145	45	50	65	180	84.29	135
11	60	45	35	35	55	55	55	48.57	25
12	50	120	35	45	35	45	55	55.00	85
13	50	70	45	75	60	45	60	57.86	30
14	40	60	40	50	60	65	95	58.57	55
15	65	60	50	25	25	100	50	53.57	75
16	60	45	35	40	30	180	50	62.86	150
17	30	30	30	65	130	80	20	55.00	110
18	45	65	65	45	40	50	25	47.86	40
19	120	30	115	50	85	40	35	67.86	90
20	40	40	55	50	25	75	55	48.57	50

while Range Charts check for consistency within the subgroups. You have to align these characteristics with your questions, or else the charts may not answer the questions of interest.

INTERNAL HOMOGENEITY

Thus, the Average and Range Chart requires a fairly sophisticated understanding of both the structure of your data and how to organize those data in order to let the two charts do their jobs. The key element in any rational subgrouping is that of internal homogeneity. When the subgroups lose their internal homogeneity the ability of the Average and Range Chart to detect process changes will suffer. This feature of the charts pushes us toward smaller rather than larger subgroups, with most charts using subgroups with fewer than 10 values.

To illustrate the Average and Range Chart I shall use the Hot Metal Transit Times shown in Table 16.1. There the transit times for 140 consecutive deliveries of Hot Metal from the blast furnace to

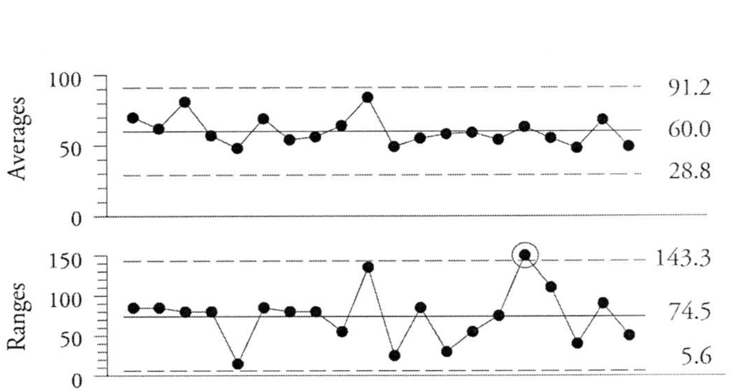

Figure 16.1: Average and Range Chart for Table 16.1

the steel furnace are shown in subgroups of size seven, along with the subgroup averages and subgroup ranges. Subgroups of size seven were used since the blast furnace averaged seven deliveries per day.

The Grand Average is 60.0 minutes, while the Average Range is 74.5 minutes. Using the scaling factors for subgroups of size seven and the formulas from Table A.2 in the Appendix, we end up with the limits shown in Figure 16.1

There we find one range value above the Upper Range Limit. This large range suggests that there is some inconsistency among the seven values in subgroup number sixteen.

If we use these data to construct an *XmR* Chart we end up with Figure 16.2. There we find 11 individual values and 13 moving ranges above their upper limits.

If one person was tracking this process using Figure 16.1, and another was tracking this process using Figure 16.2, who would be the first to know that there was a problem? While the Average Chart has tighter limits than does the *X* Chart, the inappropriate subgrouping undermines the Average Chart. Each subgroup is supposed to consist of values obtained under essentially the same conditions, yet inspection of Figure 16.2 will show that the subgroups of Table

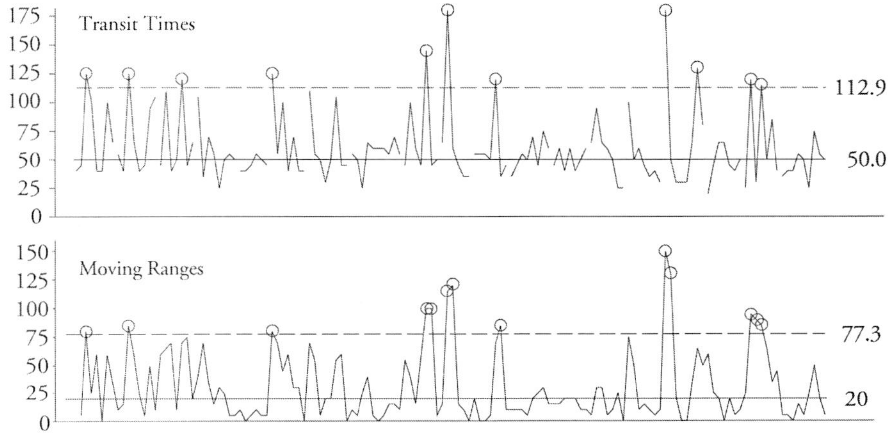

Figure 16.2: *XmR* Chart for Values in Table 16.1

16.1 do not satisfy this requirement. *When the subgroups are not homogeneous, the Average and Range Chart breaks down.* Here it was not the idea of daily subgroups that undermined the chart, but rather the fact that the process was changing within each day. Thus, even the way the process behaves can be a factor in creating a rational subgrouping.

Rational subgrouping requires judgment, process knowledge, and experience. Moreover, for many data sets there will be more than one rational subgrouping that could be used. These different rational subgroupings will answer different questions about the underlying process, and so both knowledge and judgment are required to choose between them.

Since the consequences of making the wrong decision here will be a chart that answers the wrong questions, or a chart that makes no sense at all, this is a topic that cannot be ignored. However, it is one that can be *finessed.* Instead of using subgroups, you can use the time-order sequence to place the original data on an *XmR* Chart.

It is difficult to mess up the subgrouping on an *XmR* Chart. As long as successive values are logically comparable, so that the moving ranges capture the routine variation, the *XmR* Chart will work.

SUMMARY

When you can choose both the subgroup frequency and the subgroup size you may have data that are logical candidates for an Average and Range Chart. If you can establish a rational basis for arranging these data into subgroups so that each subgroup is logically homogeneous, then the Average and Range Chart will generally provide the best analysis. But, if you are not sure about the subgrouping, then you might need to place the original data on an *XmR* Chart.

On the other hand, if you have periodically obtained data, in which each value comes with its own frequency attached, then you need to avoid the Average and Range Chart. When your data are periodically obtained any subgrouping will essentially be arbitrary. Moreover, when periodically obtained values are subgrouped you risk burying any signals within the subgroups. Since the idea of subgrouping is to bury the noise and leave the signals to occur between the subgroups, any subgrouping of periodically obtained data is, in general, a bad idea.

Finally, in practice, the potentially greater sensitivity of the Average and Range Chart does not make much difference. If you are plotting, say, five values on an *X* Chart for each single point on the Average Chart, then the multiple opportunities on the *X* Chart will tend to keep pace with the greater sensitivity of the Average Chart. By the time you detect something on the Average Chart you have already had five opportunities to detect it on the *X* Chart.

So while there are types of data where the Average and Range

Chart is the preferred chart, there is also the obstacle of creating a rational subgrouping in order to use the Average and Range Chart effectively. Until you learn how to do this, the Average and Range Chart can be worse than simply plotting the data on an *XmR* Chart.

Remember, the objective of analysis is insight. You have to discover what your process is doing. The computations are merely a means to this end. Once you have done this, you then have to communicate your discoveries to others, and you have to do this in such a way that they can take appropriate action.

The best analysis is the simplest analysis that provides the needed insight, and the *XmR* Chart is frequently the shortest distance between data and insight.

CHAPTER SEVENTEEN

WHAT ABOUT P-CHARTS?

Before the *XmR* Chart existed there were four specialty charts for individual values. These four charts are the *p*-Chart, the *np*-Chart, the *c*-Chart, and the *u*-Chart. Collectively, these four charts are commonly known as Attribute Charts. The *p*-Chart and *np*-Chart are appropriate for count-based data when those counts follow a binomial distribution. The *c*-Chart and *u*-Chart are appropriate for count-based data when those counts follow a Poisson distribution. The first of these charts, the *p*-Chart, was created by Walter Shewhart in 1924.

Data Characterized by Binomial Model Area of Opportunity = **n**		Data Characterized by Poisson Model Area of Opportunity = ***a***	
Constant **n**	Variable **n**	Constant ***a***	Variable ***a***
np-Chart for Counts	*p*-Chart for Proportions	*c*-Chart for Counts	*u*-Chart for Rates

Figure 17.1: The Four Specialty Charts for Count Data

Since count data tend to occur one value per time period, Shewhart was faced with the problem of how to create a chart for individual values. (W. J. Jennett would not have the idea of using the moving range with individual values until 1942.) While Shewhart could draw the running record, and while he could use the average for the central line, the real problem was how to construct limits that would filter out the routine variation and nothing else. Shewhart knew that the global standard deviation statistic would not work (it would be inflated by any exceptional variation that was present), so he decided to use the classic probability models for simple count data: the binomial and the Poisson distributions. Both of these models have a special characteristic that Shewhart could utilize: there were known relationships between the dispersion and the location for each of these models. By using these models, Shewhart could use his estimate of location to also obtain an estimate of dispersion. Once he had an estimate of dispersion, he could then compute a set of three-sigma limits for the chart for individual values that were appropriate for his chosen model.

This dual use of a measure of location to characterize *both* location and dispersion means that *p*-Charts, *np*-Charts, *c*-Charts, and *u*-Charts all have limits that are based upon a theoretical relationship. Hence, the Attribute Charts can all be said to use theoretical limits. If the theory is correct, then the limits will be appropriate. However, if the theory is not correct, then the limits will be inappropriate.

Many textbooks and other sources of information about SPC have conveniently forgotten this part of the logic of the Attribute Charts. They implicitly assume that *all* count-based data can be modeled by a binomial or a Poisson distribution. This is especially true of software packages. After all, when all you have is a hammer, everything looks like a nail.

Unfortunately, there are many types of count-based data that cannot be characterized by either a binomial or a Poisson distribution. When such data are placed on a *p*-Chart, *np*-Chart, *c*-Chart, or *u*-Chart the theoretical limits obtained are completely wrong.

So what are we to do? Since the problem lies in the assumption that we know the form of the relationship between location and dispersion, the solution is to estimate location and dispersion separately. And this is what the *XmR* Chart does. The average will characterize the location and serve as the central line for the *X* Chart. The Average Moving Range will characterize dispersion and serve as the basis for computing the three-sigma distance for the *X* Chart.

So what's the difference between an *X* Chart and an Attribute Chart? The *p*-Chart, *np*-Chart, *c*-Chart, and *u*-Chart will have exactly the same running record, and essentially the same central line, as the *X* Chart. Thus, the real difference between an *X* Chart and an Attribute Chart is the way the three-sigma distance is computed. While the Attribute Charts use an assumed theoretical relationship to compute a theoretical three-sigma distance, the *XmR* Chart actually measures the variation present in the data and constructs an empirical three-sigma distance.

To compare the Attribute Charts with the *XmR* Chart we shall use three examples. The first of these will use the data of Table 17.1. These values come from an accounting department which keeps track of how many of their monthly closings of departmental accounts are finished "on-time." The counts in Table 17.1 are the number of on-time closings, out of 35 closings, for each month. The *X* Chart and the *np*-Chart limits are shown in Figure 17.2.

Here both the *np*-Chart and the *X* Chart computations give essentially the same lower limit. The upper limit is not shown since it exceeds the maximum value of 35 on-time closings. The two approaches are essentially identical because these counts seem to be appropriately modeled by a binomial distribution.

Table 17.1: Number of On-Time Closings for 35 Departments

Year	Jan	Feb	Mar	Apr	May	Jun	Jul	Aug	Sep	Oct	Nov	Dec
One	32	30	32	33	32	28	30	31	32	32	32	33
Two	29	31	32	33	31	31	34	30	33	28	33	34
Three	33	33	31	29	33	30	26					

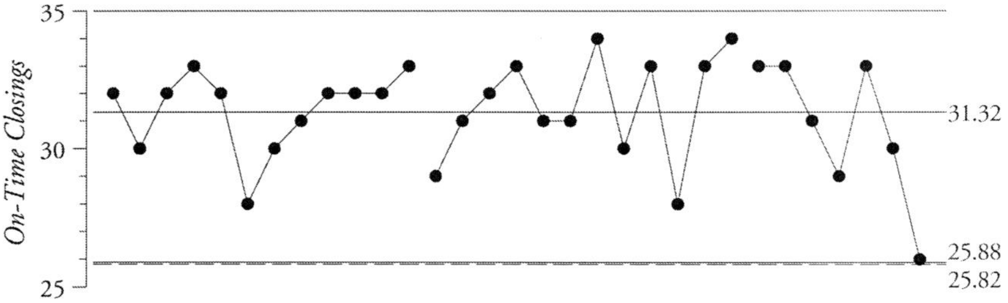

Figure 17.2: The *X* Chart and *np*-Chart for the On-Time Closing Data

If you are sophisticated enough to determine when the binomial model is appropriate, then you will know when the *np*-Chart will work, and so can use it. On the other hand, if you are not sophisticated enough to know when either the binomial or Poisson model is appropriate, then you can still use an *XmR* Chart. If the *np*-Chart, *p*-Chart, *c*-Chart, or *u*-Chart would have worked, the empirical limits of the *X* Chart will mimic the theoretical limits of the Attribute Chart, and you will not have lost anything by using the *XmR* Chart.

Our next example will use the on-time shipments for a certain plant. The data are shown in Table 17.2, while Figure 17.3 shows both the *X* Chart and the *p*-Chart for these data.

The *X* Chart shows a process with three points at or below the lower limit. The variable-width *p*-Chart limits are five times wider than the limits found using the moving ranges. No points fall outside these limits.

The discrepancy between the two sets of limits occurs here because the data of Table 17.2 do not satisfy the binomial conditions. Specifically, the probability of a shipment being on time is not the

Table 17.2: On-Time Shipments

Month	Year	Total No.	No. On-Time	On-Time %
January	01	191	176	92.1
February	01	203	186	91.6
March	01	220	202	91.8
April	01	200	183	91.5
May	01	236	215	91.1
June	01	213	194	91.1
July	01	212	191	90.1
August	01	241	215	89.2
September	01	159	143	89.9
October	01	217	197	90.8
November	01	181	165	91.2
December	01	113	103	91.2

Month	Year	Total No.	No. On-Time	On-Time %
January	02	170	155	91.2
February	02	270	246	91.1
March	02	167	151	90.4
April	02	216	196	90.7
May	02	227	206	90.7
June	02	149	136	91.3
July	02	182	167	91.8
August	02	224	206	92.0
September	02	246	225	91.5
October	02	185	170	91.9
November	02	261	239	91.6
December	02	140	128	91.4

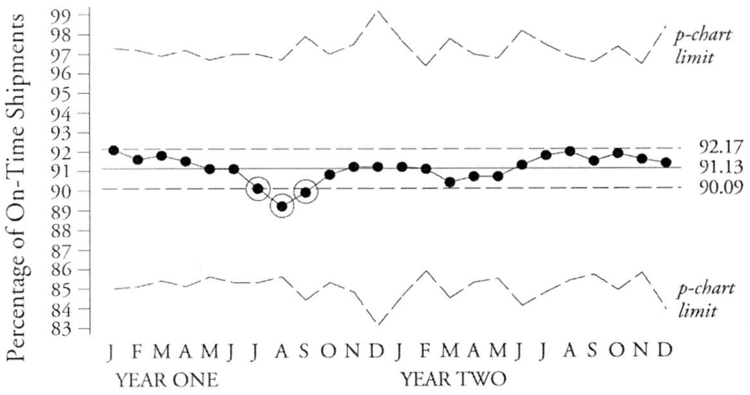

Figure 17.3: The *X* Chart and *p*-Chart for the On-Time Shipments

same for all of the shipments in any given month. (In other words, these counts simply do not behave like the drawings of colored beads from a bead bowl.)

The theoretical *p*-Chart limits in Figure 17.2 are incorrect because the binomial model is inappropriate. However, the empirical limits of the *XmR* Chart, which do not depend upon the appropriateness of a particular probability model, are correct.

Table 17.3: Premium Freight Data

Month	Year	Total No. Shipments	No. Shipped Air Freight	Percentage Air Freight
May	01	6144	374	6.09
June	01	3792	227	5.99
July	01	4792	278	5.80
August	01	7226	346	4.79
September	01	4440	161	3.63
October	01	4896	232	4.74
November	01	6019	352	5.85
December	01	4101	277	6.75

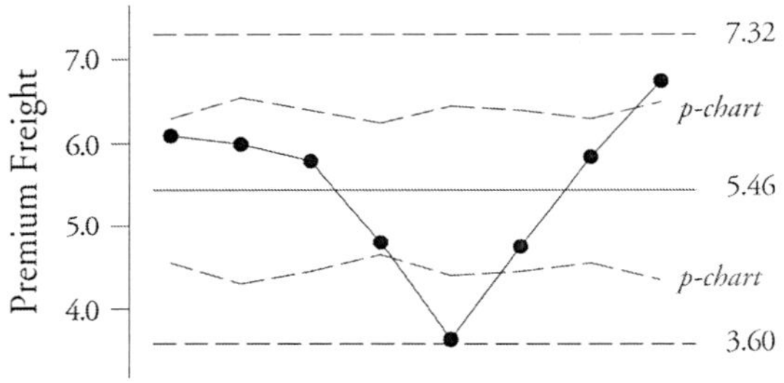

Figure 17.4: The *X* Chart and *p*-Chart for the Premium Freight Data

Our final comparison will use the data of Table 17.3. There we have the percentage of incoming shipments that were shipped by air freight for one electronics assembly plant.

The *X* Chart and the *p*-Chart limits for these data are shown in Figure 17.4. Two points fall outside the variable width *p*-Chart limits while no points fall outside the *X* Chart limits.

Figure 17.4 is typical of what happens when the area of opportunity for a count of items gets excessively large. The binomial model *requires* that all of the items in any given time period will have the same chance of possessing the attribute being counted. Here this requirement is not satisfied. With thousands of shipments each month, the probability of a shipment being shipped by air is not the same for all of the shipments. Thus, the binomial model is

Data Characterized by Binomial Model		Data Characterized by Poisson Model		Other Count-Based Data	
Area of Opportunity = n		Area of Opportunity = *a*		Constant area of opportunity	Variable area of opportunity
Constant n	Variable n	Constant *a*	Variable *a*		
np-Chart or *XmR* Chart for Counts	*p*-Chart or *XmR* Chart for Proportions	*c*-Chart or *XmR* Chart for Counts	*u*-Chart or *XmR* Chart for Rates	***XmR*** Chart for Counts	***XmR*** Chart for Rates

Figure 17.5: Choices for Charting Count-Based Data

inappropriate, and the theoretical *p*-Chart limits, which depend upon the binomial model, are incorrect. The *X* Chart limits, which here are twice as wide as the *p*-Chart limits, properly characterize both the location and dispersion of these data and are the correct limits to use.

SUMMARY

Of course, the difficulty with using the *p*-Chart, *np*-Chart, *c*-Chart, and *u*-Chart is the difficulty of determining when either the binomial or Poisson models might apply. If you do not know how to evaluate the appropriateness of these models, then you should avoid using the specialized Attribute Charts that are specifically based on these models.

In contrast to this use of theoretical models, which may or may not be correct, the *XmR* Chart provides us with empirical limits that are actually based upon the variation present in the data. This means that you can use an *XmR* Chart with count-based data anytime you wish. Since the *p*-Chart, the *np*-Chart, the *c*-Chart, and the *u*-Chart are all special cases of the chart for individual values, the *XmR* chart will mimic these specialized charts when they would be appropriate.

However, when the specialized charts are inappropriate, the *XmR* chart will still work because it uses an empirical approach rather than being based on a specific probability model. Therefore, if you do not know how to verify a particular probability model, or do not care to do so, you can still use an *XmR* chart with your count-based data.

CHAPTER EIGHTEEN

DON'T WE NEED TO REMOVE THE OUTLIERS?

Much of modern statistics is concerned with creating a model for the data. This happens both with regression techniques and with curve-fitting techniques. Since all of these models are created using mathematical algorithms, they tend to be severely affected by any values that could be described as unusual or extreme. Therefore, in order to obtain useful and appropriate models, it is often said to be necessary to polish up the data by removing the outliers.

This chapter will first illustrate the impact outliers have when we try to specify a probability model for our data. Next, the way in which this approach begs the fundamental question of homogeneity will be revealed. Finally, a variation on this erroneous approach will be described.

The data of Table 18.1 are 100 determinations of the weight of a ten-gram chrome steel standard known as NB10. The values were obtained once each week, using the same instrument, and were always obtained by one of two individuals. The weights were recorded to the nearest microgram. Since each value has the form of 9,999,xxx micrograms, the four nines at the start of each value are not shown in the table—only the last three values in the xxx positions are recorded. The values are in time order by column.

Table 18.1: 100 Weighings of NB10 (9,999,xxx micrograms)

1-10	11-20	21-30	31-40	41-50	51-60	61-70	71-80	81-90	91-100
591	602	592	597	595	596	596	588	592	599
600	597	601	600	591	594	595	594	594	593
594	593	601	590	601	593	608	591	599	588
601	598	598	599	598	595	593	600	588	625
598	599	601	593	593	589	594	592	607	591
594	601	603	577	594	590	596	596	563	594
599	600	593	594	587	590	597	599	582	602
597	599	599	594	591	590	592	596	585	594
599	595	601	598	596	599	596	592	596	597
597	598	599	595	598	598	593	594	599	596

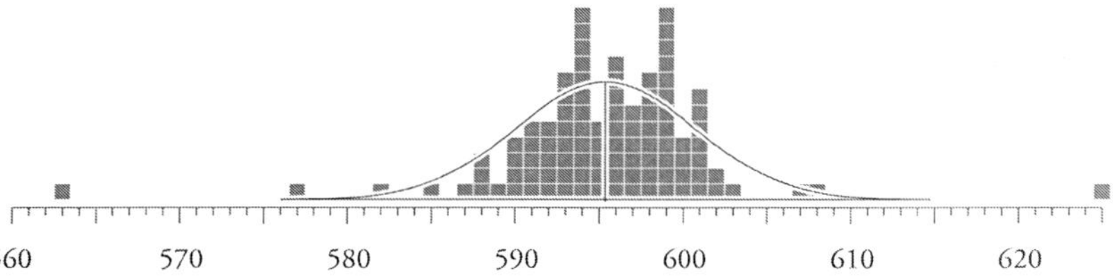

Figure 18.1: Histogram and Normal Curve for NB10 Values

If we compute the usual descriptive statistics, we find that the average of the tabled values is 595.4 micrograms, and their standard deviation statistic is 6.47 micrograms. Using these two values to define a normal distribution we would end up with the curve shown superimposed upon the histogram in Figure 18.1. Both the area under the curve and the area of the histogram are the same. Yet the curve does not really match up with the histogram. It is too heavy in the tails and not high enough in the middle.

The problem in Figure 18.1 comes from the outliers in the histogram. If we delete the seven values that look like outliers on the histogram (the three values above 606 and the four below 586) and recompute our descriptive statistics, we find the revised histogram has an average of 595.6 micrograms and a standard deviation statistic of

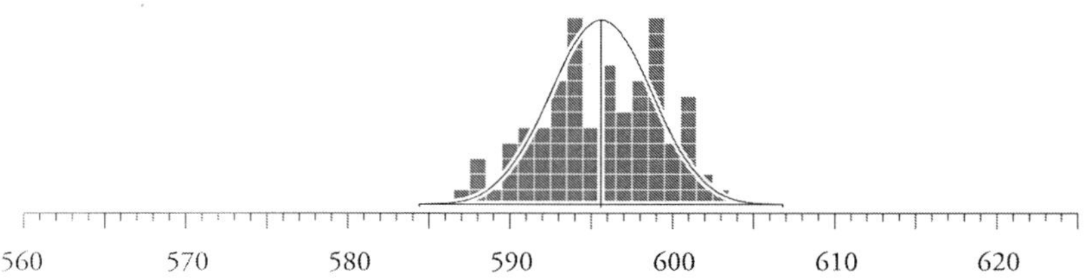

Figure 18.2: Histogram and Normal Curve for Revised NB10 Values

3.74 micrograms. Using these two values to define a normal distribution we end up with the curve shown in Figure 18.2. Now we have a much better fit between our model and our revised histogram. At this point, deleting the outliers seems to be a fairly good thing to do.

But what about the seven values we simply deleted in order to obtain this better fit between our assumed model and our revised data set? What were these values trying to tell us about this process?

The whole operation of deleting outliers to obtain a better fit between the model and the data is based upon computations which implicitly assume that the data are homogeneous. When you have outliers, this assumption becomes questionable. Recall Figure 15.5 where we learned that homogeneity is the primary question of any type of analysis.

Figure 18.3 contains the *X* Chart for the 100 values of Table 18.1 The limits are based upon the Median Moving Range of 4.0 micrograms. There is clear evidence of six upsets or changes in this process of weighing NB10. The seven "outliers" defined earlier are part of these signals, as may be seen in Figure 18.3.

Here we have a standard that is being weighed by personnel at the Bureau of Standards on a regular basis. If any set of measurements should be consistent, homogeneous, and predictable, this set should be all of these things. Yet it is not.

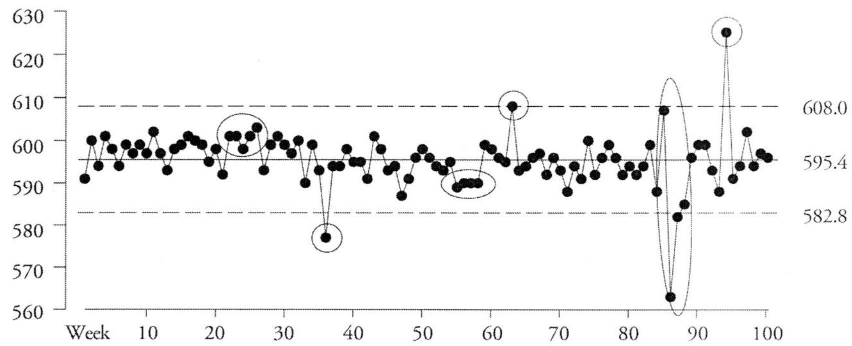

Figure 18.3: *X* Chart for 100 Weighings of NB10

The outliers that we dismissed are the signals that this set of values is not a homogeneous set of values. *From the perspective of analysis, the outliers are the most important values in the data set.* We need to understand these values rather than dismissing them. Fitting a model is premature. Here there is not one universe, but many.

DON'T THE OUTLIERS DISTORT THE LIMITS?

Do we need to remove the outliers to compute good estimates of location and dispersion? No, we don't. To see why, it is helpful to consider the impact of outliers upon the limits of a process behavior chart.

We commonly base our limits on the *average* and an *average range.* The average may be affected by some very extreme values, but this effect is usually much smaller than people expect. In the previous example some values were out of line with the bulk of the data by as much as 30 micrograms. However, the average value of approximately 595 micrograms was found by dividing 59,541 by 100. If the total of 59,541 is adjusted up or down by 30, 60, or even 90 units, it will have a very small effect upon the average. In this example deleting the outliers changed the average from 595.4 to 595.6. Thus, the average is a very robust measure of location, which is why we use it as our main statistic for location. Of course, whenever we have reason to think that the average may have been affected by the presence of several extreme values that are all on the same side, we can always use the *median* instead. Hence, while our primary measure of location is robust, we have an alternative for those cases where one is needed.

Likewise, when we compute an average range, we are once again diluting the impact of any extreme values that are present in the set of ranges. In general, a few large ranges will not have an undue impact upon the average range. However, if they do appear to have inflated the average range, we can again resort to using the *median range.* In the previous example the limits were based upon the Median Moving Range of 4.0 micrograms. This results in an estimated dispersion for the individual values of:

$$Sigma(X) = \frac{Median\ Range}{0.954} = 4.2 \text{ micrograms}$$

It is instructive to compare this value with the two values for the standard deviation statistic computed from these data. Using all 100 values from Table 18.1 we found $s = 6.47$ micrograms. Using only 93 values we found $s = 3.74$ micrograms. Thus, using all 100 values, the Median Moving Range gives an estimate for dispersion that is quite similar to the descriptive statistic computed *after the outliers had been removed.* This robustness which is built into the computations for the process behavior charts removes the need to polish the data prior to computing the limits. The computations work even in the presence of outliers and signals of exceptional variation.

DON'T WE NEED A PREDICTABLE RANGE CHART?

The fact that the computations work even in the presence of outliers is important in the light of some of the advice given in some SPC texts. These texts often warn the student to check the Range Chart before computing limits for the *X* Chart or the Average Chart. If the Range Chart is found to display evidence of unpredictable behavior, then the student is advised to avoid computing limits for the Average Chart or the *X* Chart. The idea is that signals on the Range Chart will corrupt the average range and hence corrupt the limits on the other chart. This advice is motivated by a desire to avoid using anything less than the best estimates possible. However, the objective of a process behavior chart is not *to estimate*, but rather *to characterize* the process as predictable or unpredictable. Given the conservative nature of three-sigma limits we do not need high precision in our computations. (See the Fourth Lesson in Chapter Seven.)

Thus, the advice to make sure that the Range Chart is predictable prior to computing limits for the Average Chart or the *X* Chart is just another version of the "delete the outliers" argument. These arguments are built on a misunderstanding of the objective of process behavior charts and a failure to appreciate that the computations are already robust.

SUMMARY

So, should you delete outliers before you place your data on a process behavior chart? Only if you want to throw away the most interesting and valuable part of your data!

If you fail to identify the signals of exceptional variation as such, if you assume that a collection of data is homogeneous when it is not, then you are likely to have all of your subsequent analyses and conclusions undermined.

CHAPTER NINETEEN

DON'T WE NEED GOOD MEASUREMENTS?

Who could ever be against having good measurements? Good measurements are like apple pie and motherhood. Since we all want good measurements, it sounds reasonable when people are told to check out the quality of their measurement system before putting their data on a process behavior chart. However, this is simply one more bit of advice that is completely unnecessary.

To see why this is so we will have to begin with a model for our observations. Next, we will have to look at the standard ratio for characterizing measurement error, the Intraclass Correlation Coefficient. When these are combined with the nature of three-sigma limits we will have the ability to describe how charts work with less than perfect data.

A MODEL FOR AN OBSERVATION

For our model, it should not be too hard to imagine that a single observation consists of two parts: the product value plus the measurement error.

Observation = *Product Value* + *Measurement Error*

When the measurement error component is negligible, repeated measurements of the same thing will tend to produce the same observed value. However, as the measurement error gets larger repeated measurements of the same thing will start to differ. As these repeated observations diverge, the relative utility of the measurement system will suffer.

INTRACLASS CORRELATION

We characterize the relative utility of a measurement system using the Intraclass Correlation Coefficient, ρ. This simple ratio is both theoretically sound and easy to interpret. It is defined as the ratio of two variances:

$$\rho = \frac{\text{variance of production process}}{\text{variance of product observations}}$$

This ratio is a proportion. It tells us how much of the variation in the observations can be attributed to the production process itself. When the Intraclass Correlation Coefficient is, say, 0.70, we would know that 70% of the variation in the observations would be due to variation in the production process. Since the complement of the Intraclass Correlation Coefficient, $(1-\rho)$ describes that proportion of variation in the observations that is attributable to the measurement system, we could also say that when $\rho = 0.70$, exactly 30% of the variation in the observations came from the measurement system. Hence, $(1-\rho)$ directly characterizes the extent to which measurement error intrudes into our observations.

THREE - SIGMA LIMITS

As we have seen in other chapters, three-sigma limits will filter out virtually all of the routine variation in our data. They do this reliably, and they do this without regard to where that routine variation may have originated. If you think about the fact that measurement error is always present, and then use the model from page 123, it should be apparent that measurement error will always be part of the routine variation in any set of observations.

How much of the routine variation is due to measurement error? This is defined by $(1-\rho)$. As the Intraclass Correlation Coefficient gets smaller, measurement error will comprise more and more of the routine variation, but regardless of how large $(1-\rho)$ becomes, measurement error will still be part of the routine variation. Since routine variation defines the limits, the real impact of increased measurement error upon a process behavior chart is to inflate the limits. Specifically, measurement error will inflate the limits of an *X* Chart by an amount equal to:

$$\textit{Inflation of Limits by Measurement Error} \;=\; \frac{1}{\sqrt{\rho}} - 1$$

Eventually, this inflation of the limits will have to desensitize the charts. The question is, how much measurement error is too much? To rigorously consider this question, we will need to consider how measurement error affects the ability of a process behavior chart to detect a shift in location. When we do this in the next section we will obtain a surprising answer:

Measurements will be effective on a process behavior chart until the Intraclass Correlation Coefficient drops below 0.20. This means that measurements will work on a process behavior chart as long as measurement error contributes less than 80% of the total variation.

HOW THE CHARTS WORK WITH IMPERFECT DATA

In order to incorporate the effects of all four Western Electric Detection Rules from Chapter 14, we look at the ability of an *X* Chart to detect a three-sigma shift within ten time periods of when

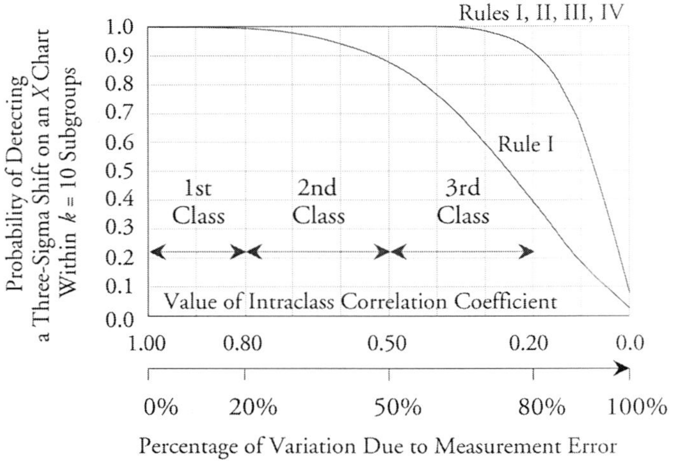

Figure 19.1: How Measurement Error Affects the *X* Chart

that shift actually occurred. The graph in Figure 19.1 is derived from tables of the power function for the *X* Chart. This graph has the values of the Intraclass Correlation Coefficient along the horizontal axis. As the Intraclass Correlation Coefficient goes from 1.00 to 0.00 the proportion of the total variation that is due to measurement error goes from 0% to 100%. The vertical axis has the probability of detecting a three-sigma shift in the production process within ten observations of when that shift occurred. The two curves show the ability of the *X* Chart to detect this shift. The upper curve is for Detection Rules One, Two, Three, and Four used together. The lower curve is for Detection Rule One alone. Both curves show that the *X* Chart maintains a high probability of detecting this shift as the measurement error increases.

First Class Monitors: When the Intraclass Correlation Coefficient is between 1.00 and 0.80 our measurement system may be said to provide a First Class Monitor. Here measurement error comprises less than 20 percent of the total variation, and there is better than a 99% chance of detecting a three-sigma shift within ten time periods.

Second Class Monitors: When the Intraclass Correlation Coefficient is between 0.80 and 0.50 our measurement system may be said to provide a Second Class Monitor. Here the measurement error will amount to between 20% and 50% of the total variation, and there will be better than a 88% chance of detecting a three-sigma shift within ten time periods with Rule One alone. When all four detection rules are used with a Second Class Monitor, we can be virtually certain that we will detect a three-sigma shift.

Third Class Monitors: When the Intraclass Correlation Coefficient is between 0.50 and 0.20 our measurement system may be said to provide a Third Class Monitor. Here the measurement error will amount to between 50% and 80% of the total variation, and yet there is still better than a 91% chance of detecting a three-sigma shift within ten time periods when using all four detection rules together.

Fourth Class Monitors: When the Intraclass Correlation Coefficient is below 0.20 our measurement system may be said to provide a Fourth Class Monitor. Here measurement error becomes so dominant that there is little product information remaining in the observations. The probabilities of detecting a three-sigma shift rapidly evaporate. Any use of a Fourth Class Monitor is an act of desperation.

Thus, measurements will be effective on a process behavior chart up to the point where measurement error amounts to more than 80% of the routine variation.

As an illustration of the truth represented by Figure 19.1 an Average and Range Chart (with $n = 8$) from a client is shown in Figure 19.2. This measurement process was right at the borderline between a Second and Third Class Monitor, with an estimated Intraclass Correlation Coefficient of 0.52. With 48% of the routine variation in

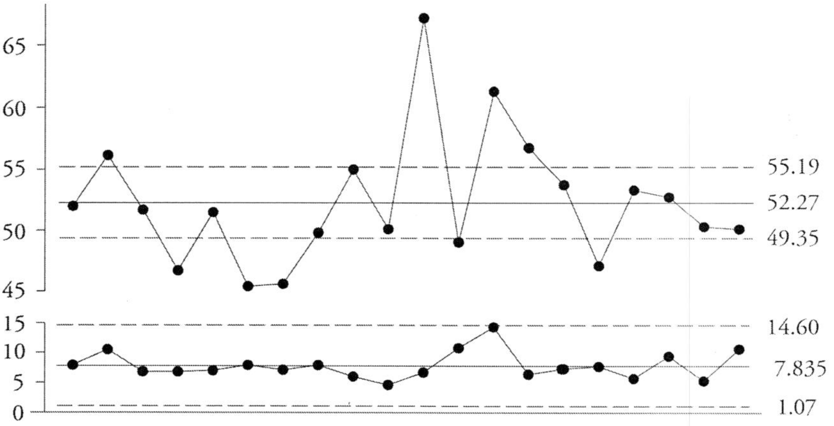

Figure 19.2: Average and Range Chart for Product 2131 Created Using a Measurement System having an Intraclass Correlation Coefficient of 52%

the observations attributable to the measurement system, and only 52% coming from the production process, the limits on the Average Chart have been inflated by the measurement error. (The limits in Figure 19.2 are about 38% wider than they would have been if the client could have used a perfect measurement system.) However, in spite of these inflated limits, there is still no question but that this process is being operated unpredictably. Here it would be a mistake to argue about the quality of the measurements. It would also be a mistake to argue about the quality of the limits. The owner of this process needs to discover the Assignable Causes that are affecting this process. Nothing else matters. If he does not take advantage of the opportunities shown on this chart, then he will continue to suffer the consequences of excess variation, scrap, and waste.

There is no way to determine the Intraclass Correlation Coefficient from Figure 19.2, but knowledge of the Intraclass Correlation Coefficient is not necessary to interpret this chart. Since excessive measurement error will tend to inflate the limits and hide signals, it is safe to interpret any signals we find as signals that occur above and beyond the masking effects of measurement error.

SUMMARY

Measurement error will inflate the limits of any process behavior chart. Yet, as shown in Figure 19.1, we will still be able to detect signals of exceptional variation whenever measurement error contributes less than 80% of the total variation. While we always like to use the best measurements possible, the process behavior chart works with imperfect data.

This means that we do not have to worry unduly about the quality of our measurements. We do not have to qualify our measurement systems before we can do business with them. As long as you have signals of exceptional variation your measurements are good enough to use on a process behavior chart. And if you attend to the signals on your process behavior charts you will be able to improve your production process. As you improve your production process you will often find that you can meet the specifications without having to resort to sorting and inspection. Until you get to the point of no longer finding any signals of exceptional variation, you do not need to check on the quality of your measurement system.

Since money, time, and effort spent on the measurement system is overhead that drains resources from your primary business, this should be good news.

CHAPTER TWENTY

THE AXIOMS OF DATA ANALYSIS

Since data analysis is different from mathematical statistics, and since moving back and forth between the different perspectives represented by the four questions listed in Chapter 15 can be confusing, it is helpful to have some axioms of data analysis laid out as fundamentals. These axioms fit into three categories: What Numbers to Compute; the Origins of Data; and Guides for Interpretation.

WHAT NUMBERS TO COMPUTE

Axiom 1
No statistic has any meaning
apart from the context for the original data.

Axiom 1 was discussed at the start of Chapter 15. While the appropriateness of a descriptive statistic depends upon the way in which it is to be used, the *meaning* of any statistic has to come from the context for the data. In particular, the data will have to display a reasonable degree of homogeneity before it will be appropriate to use the summary statistics from the data to characterize the underlying process that generated the data.

THE ORIGINS OF DATA

Axiom 2
Probability models do not generate your data.

Axiom 2 should be self-evident. However, current usage suggests that this has apparently escaped the attention of many practitioners. Probability models are mathematical descriptions of the behavior of random variables. They live on the plane of mathematical theory where measurements are frequently continuous and observations are independently and identically distributed, and usually assumed to be normally distributed as well, often with known mean and known variance. While such neat assumptions and conditions allow you to work out answers for the questions of probability theory, it is important to always remember that probability models merely approximate what happens in practice. They do not generate your data.

Axiom 3
Every histogram has finite tails.

Axiom 3 is a reminder that data sets are finite in size and extent and invariably display some level of chunkiness in the measurements. This is just one more way that real data differs from probability models, which commonly involve continuous variables and often have infinite tails.

Axiom 4
No histogram can be said
to follow a particular probability model.

Axiom 4 is actually a corollary of Axioms 2 and 3. It focuses on the fact that a probability model is, at best, a limiting characteristic of an infinite sequence of data. Therefore, *it cannot be a property of any finite portion of that sequence.* For this reason it is impossible to say that any finite data set is distributed according to a particular probability model.

But what about the Tests of Fit? Tests of Fit may allow you to say that a particular data set is *inconsistent* with a particular probability model, but they can never be used to make a positive statement that "these data are normally distributed." Such statements are impossible—inductive inference will allow us to eliminate some possibilities, but it will not allow only one unique answer.

Moreover, since histograms will always have finite tails, and since many probability models have infinite tails, it is inevitable that with enough data you will always reject any probability model you may choose. Hence G. E. P. Box's often quoted statement that "All models are wrong. Some models are more useful than others."

Axiom 5
Your data are generated by a process or system which, like everything in this world, is subject to change.

Axiom 5 is a reminder that data have a context. They are the result of some operation or process. Since the process that generates our data can change, we cannot blithely assume that our data are independently and identically distributed, nor can we define a unique probability model for our data. Even if we choose a probability model to use, and estimate the mean or the variance for that model, the fact that processes change will make both our model and the estimated parameter values inappropriate at some point.

As an example of the importance of Axioms Two through Five, we need only to look at the daily newspapers to see the consequences of ignoring these axioms. The frequency of rare events, such as floods and earthquakes, are estimated by constructing a histogram of the available data, fitting that histogram with some reasonable probability model, and then using the infinite tail of this probability model to characterize the size of a hundred-year event. The precision of this whole procedure may be seen in the fact that we have a hundred-year flood about every ten years or so. Extrapolations into the extreme tails of a probability model simply do not match reality.

GUIDES FOR INTERPRETATION

Axiom 6
All outliers are *prima facie* evidence of nonhomogeneity.

While the procedures of statistical inference can be "sharpened up" by deleting any outliers contained in the data, the very existence of the outliers is evidence of a lack of homogeneity. Since the techniques of statistics are predicated upon the existence of a universe, and a lack of homogeneity undermines this assumption, it is critical to understand the source of the outliers rather than to simply assume that they do not exist. Whenever a process is being operated up to its full potential it will produce a homogeneous data stream. Hence, rather than being a problem, outliers represent opportunities to solve problems.

Axiom 7
Every data set contains noise.
Some data sets also contain signals.
Before you can detect the signals within your data
you must filter out the noise.

Variation comes in two flavors—routine variation and exceptional variation. Until you know how to separate the exceptional from the routine you will be hopelessly confused in any attempt at analysis. This axiom is so important that it was singled out as the "Second Principle for Understanding Data" in *Understanding Variation.*

A failure to understand this axiom is the hallmark of numerical naiveté. Ignore Axiom Seven and you too can become the source of endless confusion and disinformation.

Axiom 8
You must *detect* a difference
before you can legitimately *estimate* that difference,
and only then can you
***assess the practical importance* of that difference.**

When the noise of routine variation obscures a difference it is a mistake to try to estimate that difference. With statistical techniques a detectable difference is one that is commonly referred to as "significant." Statistical significance has nothing to do with the practical importance of a difference, but merely with whether or not it is detectable. If it is detectable, then you can obtain a reliable estimate of that difference. If a difference is not detectable and you attempt to estimate it anyway, you will be lucky to end up with the right sign, much less any correct digits. When the routine variation obscures a difference, it cannot be estimated from the data with any reliability. Finally, only after detecting and estimating a difference can you assess whether or not that difference is of any practical importance. Try it in any other order, and you are likely to be interpreting noise.

SUMMARY

As a result of all this, we can say that statistical techniques will provide approximate, yet reliable, ways of separating potential signals from probable noise. This is the unifying theme of all techniques for statistical analysis. Data analysis is ultimately concerned with filtering out the noise of routine variation in a systematic manner that will stand up to the scrutiny of skeptics. This filtration does not have to be perfect. It just needs to be good enough to let us identify the potential signals within our data.

At the same time, using the theoretical relationships developed by means of probability theory will result in inference techniques that are reasonable and that will allow the appropriate level of filtration to occur. While statistical techniques may only be approximate, they are more reliable, more precise, and more reproducible than the alternative of *ad hoc*, experience-based interpretations of the data.

Everything you do under the heading of data analysis should be governed by the preceding axioms. Otherwise you risk the hazards of missing signals and being misled by noise.

Process behavior charts have a fine ancestry of highbrow statistical theorems. Yet for Shewhart, this was not enough to justify their use. He also required that they would work in practice. Process behavior charts have been thoroughly proven the world over. They provide an empirical approach to answering the basic question of data analysis: Are these data homogeneous, or do they display evidence of having come from a process that was changing? Until you answer this question, all other questions about, comments on, and interpretations of the data are moot.

APPENDICES

FOR FURTHER READING

The following citations identify those places in some of my other books where the topics of this book are addressed.

CHAPTER ONE
THE TWO MISTAKES OF DATA ANALYSIS

Understanding Variation, pages 30-31, 53-54.
Making Sense of Data, pages 96-98.
Understanding Statistical Process Control, page *xi*.
Advanced Topics in Statistical Process Control, pages 14, 127.

CHAPTER TWO
TWO TYPES OF DATA

EMP III, Evaluating the Measurement Process, pages 7-8.

CHAPTER THREE
THE ORIGIN AND STRUCTURE OF VARIATION

The Six Sigma Practitioner's Guide to Data Analysis, pages 235-241.
Normality and the Process Behavior Chart, pages 41-48.

CHAPTER FOUR
THREE QUESTIONS FOR SUCCESS

Making Sense of Data, pages 5-6, 33-34.
Understanding Statistical Process Control, pages 7-11, 290.

CHAPTER FIVE
WHERE DO THE SCALING FACTORS COME FROM?

Making Sense of Data, pages 165-166.
Understanding Statistical Process Control, pages 236-249.
Advanced Topics in Statistical Process Control, pages 418-439.
The Six Sigma Practitioner's Guide to Data Analysis, pages 42-43.
Normality and the Process Behavior Chart, pages 57-63.

CHAPTER SIX
WHY NOT JUST USE THE STANDARD DEVIATION STATISTIC?

Making Sense of Data, pages 161-162.
Understanding Statistical Process Control, pages 56-59, 214-215.
The Six Sigma Practitioner's Guide to Data Analysis, pages 19-38.

CHAPTER SEVEN
DON'T WE NEED NORMAL DATA?

Understanding Statistical Process Control, pages 65-77.
Advanced Topics in Statistical Process Control, pages 116-126.
Normality and the Process Behavior Chart, pages 77-90.

CHAPTER EIGHT
BUT THE SOFTWARE TRANSFORMS THE DATA!

Advanced Topics in Statistical Process Control, page 28.
Normality and the Process Behavior Chart, pages 38-39, 77-90.

CHAPTER NINE
WHY USE THREE - SIGMA LIMITS?

Making Sense of Data, pages 96-97.
Understanding Statistical Process Control, pages 60-65.
Advanced Topics in Statistical Process Control, pages 115-120.
Normality and the Process Behavior Chart, pages 77-96.

CHAPTER TEN
HOW MANY DATA DO I NEED FOR LIMITS?

Understanding Variation, pages 114-117.
Making Sense of Data, pages 129, 137-138.

CHAPTER ELEVEN
WHEN DO I NEED TO REVISE THE LIMITS?

Making Sense of Data, pages 121-140.
Understanding Statistical Process Control, pages 226-230.
Advanced Topics in Statistical Process Control, page 122.

CHAPTER TWELVE
BUT THE LIMITS ARE TOO WIDE!

Making Sense of Data, pages 150, 237-255.
Understanding Statistical Process Control, pages 285-307.

CHAPTER THIRTEEN
WHEN DO WE USE A MEDIAN MOVING RANGE?

Making Sense of Data, pages 145-151.
Understanding Statistical Process Control, pages 226-228.
Advanced Topics in Statistical Process Control, pages 88-91.

CHAPTER FOURTEEN
WHAT CAN BE CONSIDERED A SIGNAL?

Making Sense of Data, pages 108-112.
Understanding Statistical Process Control, pages 90-97.
Advanced Topics in Statistical Process Control, pages 135-140.
The Six Sigma Practitioner's Guide to Data Analysis, pages 52-57.
EMP III, Evaluating the Measurement Process, page 245.

CHAPTER FIFTEEN
WHY A PROCESS BEHAVIOR CHART IS THE FIRST STEP IN DATA ANALYSIS

Understanding Variation, pages 29-31.
Making Sense of Data, pages 95-99.
Understanding Statistical Process Control, pages 4-11.
Advanced Topics in Statistical Process Control, pages 18-19.
The Six Sigma Practitioner's Guide to Data Analysis, pages 3-12.

CHAPTER SIXTEEN
WHEN DO WE USE SUBGROUPED DATA?

Making Sense of Data, pages 270-277.
Understanding Statistical Process Control, pages 217-218.
Advanced Topics in Statistical Process Control, page 236.

CHAPTER SEVENTEEN
WHAT ABOUT P - CHARTS?

Understanding Variation, page 138.
Making Sense of Data, pages 199-233.
Understanding Statistical Process Control, pages 255-280.
Advanced Topics in Statistical Process Control, pages 251-271.
The Six Sigma Practitioner's Guide to Data Analysis, pages 175-206.

CHAPTER EIGHTEEN
DON'T WE NEED TO REMOVE THE OUTLIERS?

Understanding Statistical Process Control, pages 226-230.
Advanced Topics in Statistical Process Control, page 84.
The Six Sigma Practitioner's Guide to Data Analysis, pages 15, 186.

CHAPTER NINETEEN
DON'T WE NEED GOOD MEASUREMENTS?

Understanding Statistical Process Control, pages 151-154.
The Six Sigma Practitioner's Guide to Data Analysis, pages 320-323.
EMP III, Evaluating the Measurement Process, pages 195-216.

CHAPTER TWENTY
THE AXIOMS OF DATA ANALYSIS

Understanding Variation, pages 13, 30.
The Six Sigma Practitioner's Guide to Data Analysis, pages 12-16.

TABLES FOR CONSTRUCTING CHARTS

Table A.1: Bias Correction Factors

n	c_4	d_2	d_3	d_4	n	c_4	d_2	d_3	d_4
2	.7979	1.128	0.8525	0.954	21	.9876	3.778	0.7242	3.730
3	.8862	1.693	0.8884	1.588	22	.9882	3.819	0.7199	3.771
4	.9213	2.059	0.8798	1.978	23	.9887	3.858	0.7159	3.811
5	.9400	2.326	0.8641	2.257	24	.9892	3.895	0.7121	3.847
6	.9515	2.534	0.8480	2.472	25	.9896	3.931	0.7084	3.883
7	.9594	2.704	0.8332	2.645	30	.9915	4.086	0.6927	4.037
8	.9650	2.847	0.8198	2.791	35	.9927	4.213	0.6799	4.166
9	.9693	2.970	0.8078	2.915	40	.9936	4.322	0.6692	4.274
10	.9727	3.078	0.7971	3.024	45	.9943	4.415	0.6601	4.372
11	.9754	3.173	0.7873	3.121	50	.9949	4.498	0.6521	4.450
12	.9776	3.258	0.7785	3.207	55	.9954	4.572	0.6452	4.521
13	.9794	3.336	0.7704	3.285	60	.9957	4.639	0.6389	4.591
14	.9810	3.407	0.7630	3.356	65	.9961	4.699	0.6333	4.649
15	.9823	3.472	0.7562	3.422	70	.9964	4.755	0.6283	4.707
16	.9835	3.532	0.7499	3.482	75	.9966	4.806	0.6236	4.757
17	.9845	3.588	0.7441	3.538	80	.9968	4.854	0.6194	4.806
18	.9854	3.640	0.7386	3.591	85	.9970	4.898	0.6154	4.849
19	.9862	3.689	0.7335	3.640	90	.9972	4.939	0.6118	4.892
20	.9869	3.735	0.7287	3.686	100	.9975	5.015	0.6052	4.968

Given k subgroups of size n, the within-subgroup measure of dispersion for X and R will be obtained using one of the following:

$$Sigma(X) = \frac{\bar{s}}{c_4} \quad \text{or} \quad \frac{\bar{R}}{d_2} \quad \text{or} \quad \frac{\tilde{R}}{d_4}$$

$$Sigma(R) = \frac{d_3\,\bar{R}}{d_2} \quad \text{or} \quad \frac{d_3\,\tilde{R}}{d_4}$$

These values are automatically incorporated into the formulas given in the following tables.

Table A.2: Average and Range Charts
Scaling Factors for Using the Average Range, $\bar{R}$

Given k subgroups, each with n observations,
with Grand Average, $\bar{\bar{X}}$ and Average Range, $\bar{R}$
use the tabled constants with the formulas to obtain
- limits for Subgroup Averages,
- limits for Subgroup Ranges, or
- Natural Process Limits for X.

n	A_2	D_3	D_4	E_2
2	1.880	--	3.268	2.660
3	1.023	--	2.574	1.772
4	0.729	--	2.282	1.457
5	0.577	--	2.114	1.290
6	0.483	--	2.004	1.184
7	0.419	0.076	1.924	1.109
8	0.373	0.136	1.864	1.054
9	0.337	0.184	1.816	1.010
10	0.308	0.223	1.777	0.975
11	0.285	0.256	1.744	0.945
12	0.266	0.283	1.717	0.921
13	0.249	0.307	1.693	0.899
14	0.235	0.328	1.672	0.881
15	0.223	0.347	1.653	0.864

Table A.2: Average and Range Charts Continued

Formulas for Using the Average Range, $\bar{R}$

Limits for Subgroup Averages will be:

$$UAL_{\bar{X}} = \bar{\bar{X}} + A_2\,\bar{R}$$

$$CL_{\bar{X}} = \bar{\bar{X}}$$

$$LAL_{\bar{X}} = \bar{\bar{X}} - A_2\,\bar{R}$$

Limits for Subgroup Ranges will be:

$$URL_R = D_4\,\bar{R}$$

$$CL_R = \bar{R}$$

$$LRL_R = D_3\,\bar{R}$$

If needed, Natural Process Limits for Individual Values
may be obtained using the following:

$$UNPL_X = \bar{\bar{X}} + E_2\,\bar{R}$$

$$CL_X = \bar{\bar{X}}$$

$$LNPL_X = \bar{\bar{X}} - E_2\,\bar{R}$$

The Scaling Factors above may be expressed in terms of the bias correction factors as:

$$A_2 = \frac{3}{d_2\sqrt{n}}$$

$$D_3 = \left[\,1 - \frac{3\,d_3}{d_2}\,\right] \qquad D_4 = \left[\,1 + \frac{3\,d_3}{d_2}\,\right]$$

$$E_2 = \frac{3}{d_2}$$

Table A.3: Average and Standard Deviation Charts
Scaling Factors for Using the Average Standard Deviation, $\bar{s}$

Given k subgroups, each with n observations,
with Grand Average, $\bar{\bar{X}}$, and Average Standard Deviation, $\bar{s}$
use the tabled constants with the formulas to obtain

- limits for Subgroup Averages,
- limits for Subgroup Standard Deviations, or
- Natural Process Limits for individual values.

n	A_3	B_3	B_4	E_3
2	2.659	--	3.267	3.760
3	1.954	--	2.568	3.385
4	1.628	--	2.266	3.256
5	1.427	--	2.089	3.191
6	1.287	0.030	1.970	3.153
7	1.182	0.118	1.882	3.127
8	1.099	0.185	1.815	3.109
9	1.032	0.239	1.761	3.095
10	0.975	0.284	1.716	3.084
11	0.927	0.322	1.678	3.076
12	0.886	0.354	1.646	3.069
13	0.850	0.382	1.619	3.063
14	0.817	0.407	1.593	3.058
15	0.789	0.428	1.572	3.054

Table A.3: Average and Standard Deviation Charts Continued
Formulas for Using the Average Standard Deviation, $\bar{s}$

Limits for Subgroup Averages will be:

$$UAL_{\bar{X}} = \bar{\bar{X}} + A_3\,\bar{s}$$

$$CL_{\bar{X}} = \bar{\bar{X}}$$

$$LAL_{\bar{X}} = \bar{\bar{X}} - A_3\,\bar{s}$$

Limits for Subgroup Standard Deviations will be:

$$USDL_S = B_4\,\bar{s}$$

$$CL_S = \bar{s}$$

$$LSDL_S = B_3\,\bar{s}$$

If needed, Natural Process Limits for Individual Values may be obtained using the following:

$$UNPL_X = \bar{\bar{X}} + E_3\,\bar{s}$$

$$CL_X = \bar{\bar{X}}$$

$$LNPL_X = \bar{\bar{X}} - E_3\,\bar{s}$$

The Scaling Factors above may be expressed in terms of the bias correction factors as:

$$A_3 = \frac{3}{c_4\sqrt{n}}$$

$$B_3 = 1 - \frac{3}{c_4}\sqrt{1-(c_4)^2} \qquad B_4 = 1 + \frac{3}{c_4}\sqrt{1-(c_4)^2}$$

$$E_3 = \frac{3}{c_4}$$

Table A.4
Charts for Individual Values and Moving Ranges

When a *time series* has a logical subgroup size of $n = 1$ we can plot the individual values and use a two-point moving range to measure the dispersion. The Average Moving Range or the Median Moving Range may then be used to compute the Natural Process Limits for the individual values and the Upper Range Limit for the moving ranges according to the formulas:

$$UNPL_X = \bar{X} + E_2 \bar{R} \quad \text{or} \quad \bar{X} + E_5 \tilde{R}$$

$$CL_X = \bar{X}$$

$$LNPL_X = \bar{X} - E_2 \bar{R} \quad \text{or} \quad \bar{X} - E_5 \tilde{R}$$

$$URL_R = D_4 \bar{R} \quad \text{or} \quad D_6 \tilde{R}$$

$$CL_R = \bar{R} \quad \text{or} \quad \tilde{R}$$

For two-period moving ranges these constants are:

$$E_2 = \frac{3}{d_2} = 2.660 \qquad E_5 = \frac{3}{d_4} = 3.145$$

$$D_4 = \left[1 + \frac{3\,d_3}{d_2} \right] = 3.267 \qquad D_6 = \frac{d_2 + 3\,d_3}{d_4} = 3.863$$

where d_2, d_3 and d_4 are the bias correction factors for $n = 2$.

Comments for Table A.4
Charts for Individual Values and Moving Ranges

- Successive values on the *X* chart must be logically comprable in order for the moving ranges to capture the routine variation.
- If the individual values are *known* to come from different cause systems, as would be the case in a sequence of experimental runs, then the moving ranges may not be used to construct control limits even when the data constitute a time series.
- If the data do not come from a time series, i.e., if the individual values do not possess a definite and known time order, then the use of a moving range to measure the dispersion of the data is essentially arbitrary because the order of the data is arbitrary.
- Moving ranges which fall above the upper range limit may be taken as indications of a potential break in the time series—some sudden shift which is so large that it is unlikely to have occurred by chance.
- There is no advantage to using any other measure of dispersion besides a two-point moving range. Moving ranges based on three or more values will be harder to compute and less efficient than the two-point moving ranges. Mean square successive differences will be harder to compute and more prone to being inflated by extreme values while being no more efficient than the two-point moving range. Global measures of dispersion beg the question of statistical control by making a strong assumption that the data are completely homogeneous, and so they can never be properly used to compute limits for individual values.

INDEX